Grade 3

Scott Foresman
Leveled Reader
Teaching Guide

PEARSON
Scott Foresman

Editorial Offices: Glenview, Illinois • Parsippany, New Jersey • New York, New York
Sales Offices: Boston, Massachusetts • Duluth, Georgia • Glenview, Illinois
Coppell, Texas • Sacramento, California • Mesa, Arizona

ISBN: 0-328-16922-6

4 5 6 7 8 9 10 V084 12 11 10 09 08 07 06

Table of Contents

LEVELED READER TITLE	Instruction	Comprehension Practice	Vocabulary Practice
Mr. Post's Class	12–13	14	15
What's Money All About?	16–17	18	19
Maggie McGee and Me at the Mint	20–21	22	23
Mr. Grim and the Goose That Laid Golden Eggs	24–25	26	27
Pizza With a Twist	28–29	30	31
Penguins On Parade	32–33	34	35
The Song Makers Go to Salem	36–37	38	39
Collecting Dreams	40–41	42	43
The Magic of Coyote	44–45	46	47
Houses Past and Present	48–49	50	51
Nicky's Meadow	52–53	54	55
Star Tracks	56–57	58	59
Follow Me! How People Track Animals	60–61	62	63
Whales and Other Animal Wonders	64–65	66	67
Earth Movement	68–69	70	71
Special Talents, Extraordinary Lives	72–73	74	75
Fastest, Longest, Biggest, Lightest: The *Guinness World Records* Story	76–77	78	79
A Gem of a Tale!	80–81	82	83

© Pearson Education

Graphic Organizers

Introduction

Scott Foresman *Reading Street* provides over 600 leveled readers that help children become better readers and build a lifelong love of reading. The *Reading Street* leveled readers are engaging texts that help children practice critical reading skills and strategies. They also provide opportunities to build vocabulary, understand concepts, and develop reading fluency.

The leveled readers were developed to be age-appropriate and appealing to children at each grade level. The leveled readers consist of engaging texts in a variety of genres, including fantasy, folk tales, realistic fiction, historical fiction, and narrative and expository nonfiction. To better address real-life reading skills that children will encounter in testing situations and beyond, a higher percentage of nonfiction texts is provided at each grade.

USING THE LEVELED READERS

You can use the leveled readers to meet the diverse needs of your children. Consider using the readers to

- practice critical skills and strategies
- build fluency
- build vocabulary and concepts
- build background for the main selections in the student book
- provide a variety of reading experiences, e.g., shared, group, individual, take-home, readers' theater

GUIDED READING APPROACH

The *Reading Street* leveled readers are leveled according to Guided Reading criteria by experts trained in Guided Reading. The Guided Reading levels increase in difficulty within a grade level and across grade levels. In addition to leveling according to Guided Reading criteria, the instruction provided in the *Leveled Reader Teaching Guide* is compatible with Guided Reading instruction. An instructional routine is provided for each leveled reader. This routine is most effective when working with individual children or small groups.

MANAGING THE CLASSROOM

When using the leveled readers with individuals or small groups, you'll want to keep the other children engaged in meaningful, independent learning tasks. Establishing independent work stations throughout the classroom and child routines for these work stations can help you manage the rest of the class while you work with individuals or small groups. Possible work stations include Listening, Phonics, Vocabulary, Independent Reading, and Cross-Curricular. For classroom management, create a work board that lists the work stations and which children should be at each station. Provide instructions at each station that detail the tasks to be accomplished. Update the board and alert children when they should rotate to a new station. For additional support for managing your classroom, see the *Reading Street Centers Survival Kit*.

USING THE LEVELED READER TEACHING GUIDE

The *Leveled Reader Teaching Guide* provides an instruction plan for each leveled reader based on the same instructional routine.

INTRODUCE THE BOOK The Introduction includes suggestions for creating interest in the text by discussing the title and author, building background, and previewing the book and its features.

READ THE BOOK Before students begin reading the book, have them set purposes for reading and discuss how they can use the reading strategy as they read. Determine how you want students in a particular group to read the text, softly or silently, to a specific point or the entire text. Then use the Comprehension Questions to provide support as needed and to assess comprehension.

REVISIT THE BOOK The Reader Response questions provide opportunities for students to demonstrate their understanding of the text, the target comprehension skill, and vocabulary. The Response Options require students to revisit the text to respond to what they've read and to move beyond the text to explore related content.

SKILL WORK The Skill Work box provides instruction and practice for the target skill and strategy and selection vocabulary. Instruction for an alternate comprehension skill allows teachers to provide additional skill instruction and practice for students.

USING THE GRAPHIC ORGANIZERS

Graphic organizers in blackline-master format can be found on pages 132–152. These can be used as overhead transparencies or as student worksheets.

ASSESSING PERFORMANCE

Use the assessment forms that begin on page 6 to make notes about your students' reading skills, use of reading strategies, and general reading behaviors.

MEASURE FLUENT READING (pp. 6–7) Provides directions for measuring a student's fluency, based on words correct per minute (wcpm), and reading accuracy using a running record.

OBSERVATION CHECKLIST (p. 8) Allows you to note the regularity with which students demonstrate their understanding and use of reading skills and strategies.

STUDENT SELF-ASSESSMENT (p. 9) Helps students identify their own areas of strength and areas where they need further work. This form (About My Reading) encourages them to list steps they can take to become better readers and to set goals as readers. Suggest that students share their self-assessment notes with their families so that family members can work with them more effectively to practice their reading skills and strategies at home.

READING STRATEGY ASSESSMENT (p. 10) Provides criteria for evaluating each student's proficiency as a strategic reader.

PROGRESS REPORT (p. 11) Provides a means to track a student's book-reading progress over a period of time by noting the level at which a student reads and his or her accuracy at that level. Reading the chart from left to right gives you a visual model of how quickly a student is making the transition from one level to the next. Share these reports with parents or guardians to help them see how their child's reading is progressing.

Measure
Fluent Reading

Taking a Running Record

A running record is an assessment of a student's oral reading accuracy and oral reading fluency. Reading accuracy is based on the number of words read correctly. Reading fluency is based on the reading rate (the number of words correct per minute) and the degree to which a student reads with a "natural flow."

How to Measure Reading Accuracy

1. Choose a grade-level text of about 80 to 120 words that is unfamiliar to the student.
2. Make a copy of the text for yourself. Make a copy for the student or have the student read aloud from a book.
3. Give the student the text and have the student read aloud. (You may wish to record the student's reading for later evaluation.)
4. On your copy of the text, mark any miscues or errors the student makes while reading. See the running record sample on page 7, which shows how to identify and mark miscues.
5. Count the total number of words in the text and the total number of errors made by the student. Note: If a student makes the same error more than once, such as mispronouncing the same word multiple times, count it as one error. Self-corrections do not count as actual errors. Use the following formula to calculate the percentage score, or accuracy rate:

$$\frac{\text{Total Number of Words} - \text{Total Number of Errors}}{\text{Total Number of Words}} \times 100 = \text{percentage score}$$

Interpreting the Results

- A student who reads **95–100%** of the words correctly is reading at an **independent level** and may need more challenging text.
- A student who reads **90–94%** of the words correctly is reading at an **instructional level** and will likely benefit from guided instruction.
- A student who reads **89%** or fewer of the words correctly is reading at a **frustrational level** and may benefit most from targeted instruction with lower-level texts and intervention.

How to Measure Reading Rate (WCPM)

1. Follow Steps 1–3 above.
2. Note the exact times when the student begins and finishes reading.
3. Use the following formula to calculate the number of words correct per minute (WCPM):

$$\frac{\text{Total Number of Words Read Correctly}}{\text{Total Number of Seconds}} \times 60 = \text{words correct per minute}$$

Interpreting the Results

By the end of the year, a third-grader should be reading approximately 110–120 WCPM.

Running Record Sample

Running Record Sample

Dana had recently begun volunteering at the animal rescue shelter where her mom worked as a veterinarian. The shelter was (just) across the bay from their house.

Dana was learning many *different* jobs at the shelter. She fed the dogs and cleaned their cages. She played catch with the dogs in the shelter's backyard. Dana's favorite *job*, however, was introducing people to the dogs waiting for adoption. Whenever a dog found a new home, Dana was (sc) especially pleased!

The road to the shelter crossed over the bay. Dana looked for boats in the channel, but there were none. Dana's mom turned on the radio to ~~listen~~ *hear* to the news as they drove. The weather reporter announced that a blizzard might hit some parts of the state.

—From *A Day with the Dogs*
On-Level Reader 3.3.4

Notations

Accurate Reading
The student reads a word correctly.

Omission
The student omits words or word parts.

Hesitation
The student hesitates over a word, and the teacher provides the word. Wait several seconds before telling the student what the word is.

Mispronunciation/Misreading
The student pronounces or reads a word incorrectly.

Self-correction
The student reads a word incorrectly but then corrects the error. Do not count self-corrections as actual errors. However, noting self-corrections will help you identify words the student finds difficult.

Insertion
The student inserts words or parts of words that are not in the text.

Substitution
The student substitutes words or parts of words for the words in the text.

Running Record Results
Total Number of Words: **126**
Number of Errors: **5**

Reading Time: **64 seconds**

▶ **Reading Accuracy**
$\frac{126 - 5}{126} \times 100 = 96.032 = 96\%$

Accuracy Percentage Score: **96%**

▶ **Reading Rate—WCPM**
$\frac{121}{64} \times 60 = 113.44 = 113$ words correct per minute

Reading Rate: **113 WCPM**

Observation Checklist

Student's Name _____ Date _____

Behaviors Observed	Always (Proficient)	Usually (Fluent)	Sometimes (Developing)	Rarely (Novice)
Uses prior knowledge and preview to understand what book is about				
Makes predictions and checks them while reading				
Uses context clues to figure out meanings of new words				
Uses phonics and syllabication to decode words				
Self-corrects while reading				
Reads at an appropriate reading rate				
Reads with appropriate intonation and stress				
Uses fix-up strategies				
Identifies story elements: character, setting, plot, theme				
Summarizes plot or main ideas accurately				
Uses target comprehension skill to understand the text better				
Responds thoughtfully about the text				

Reading Behaviors and Attitudes

Enjoys listening to stories				
Chooses reading as a free-time activity				
Reads with sustained interest and attention				
Participates in discussion about books				

General Comments

About My Reading

Name _____ Date _____

1. **Compared with earlier in the year, I am enjoying reading**

   ☐ more   ☐ less   ☐ about the same

2. **When I read now, I understand**

   ☐ more than I used to   ☐ about the same as I used to

3. **One thing that has helped me with my reading is**

   _____

   _____

   _____

4. **One thing that could make me a better reader is**

   _____

   _____

   _____

5. **Here is one selection or book that I really enjoyed reading:**

   _____

   _____

6. **Here are some reasons why I liked it:**

   _____

   _____

   _____

   _____

   _____

   _____

Reading Strategy Assessment

Student _____ Date _____

Teacher _____

		Proficient	Developing	Emerging	Not showing trait
Building Background Comments:	Previews	☐	☐	☐	☐
	Asks questions	☐	☐	☐	☐
	Predicts	☐	☐	☐	☐
	Activates prior knowledge	☐	☐	☐	☐
	Sets own purposes for reading	☐	☐	☐	☐
	Other:	☐	☐	☐	☐
Comprehension Comments:	Retells/summarizes	☐	☐	☐	☐
	Questions, evaluates ideas	☐	☐	☐	☐
	Relates to self/other texts	☐	☐	☐	☐
	Paraphrases	☐	☐	☐	☐
	Rereads/reads ahead for meaning	☐	☐	☐	☐
	Visualizes	☐	☐	☐	☐
	Uses decoding strategies	☐	☐	☐	☐
	Uses vocabulary strategies	☐	☐	☐	☐
	Understands key ideas of a text	☐	☐	☐	☐
	Other:	☐	☐	☐	☐
Fluency Comments:	Adjusts reading rate	☐	☐	☐	☐
	Reads for accuracy	☐	☐	☐	☐
	Uses expression	☐	☐	☐	☐
	Other:	☐	☐	☐	☐
Connections Comments:	Relates text to self	☐	☐	☐	☐
	Relates text to text	☐	☐	☐	☐
	Relates text to world	☐	☐	☐	☐
	Other:	☐	☐	☐	☐
Self-Assessment Comments:	Is aware of: Strengths	☐	☐	☐	☐
	Needs	☐	☐	☐	☐
	Improvement/achievement	☐	☐	☐	☐
	Sets and implements learning goals	☐	☐	☐	☐
	Maintains logs, records, portfolio	☐	☐	☐	☐
	Works with others	☐	☐	☐	☐
	Shares ideas and materials	☐	☐	☐	☐
	Other:	☐	☐	☐	☐

Progress Report

Student's Name _____

At the top of the chart, record the book title, its grade/unit/week (for example, 1.2.3), and the student's accuracy percentage. See page 6 for measuring fluency, calculating accuracy and reading rates. At the bottom of the chart, record the date you took the running record. In the middle of the chart, make an X in the box across from the level of the student's reading—frustrational level (below 89% accuracy), instructional level (90–94% accuracy), or independent level (95–100% accuracy). Record the reading rate (wcpm) in the next row.

Book Title						
Grade/Unit/Week						
Reading Accuracy Percentage						
LEVEL — Frustrational (89% or below)						
LEVEL — Instructional (90–94%)						
LEVEL — Independent (95% or above)						
Reading Rate (WCPM)						
Date						

Mr. Post's Class

SUMMARY The new school year is underway, and one class has a new teacher, Mr. Post. His experience as a summer volunteer inspires him and his students to develop a yearlong community volunteer project through which students offer their time and skills to members of the community.

LESSON VOCABULARY

community	enthusiasm
labor	mural
nonprofit	organization
reporter	sign-up
success	volunteer

INTRODUCE THE BOOK

INTRODUCE THE TITLE AND AUTHOR Discuss with students the title and the author of *Mr. Post's Class*. Ask them to look at the cover illustration and talk about how it might relate to the title. Ask: Who is the man in the illustration, and what is he doing? Why is his name on the chalkboard?

BUILD BACKGROUND Discuss community service and volunteering. Ask: Why do people volunteer? Have you or members of your family volunteered? Have you ever been helped by volunteers?

ELL Ask students to discuss what aspects of starting a new school year are exciting and which are difficult. Ask: How can others help students who are not native English speakers?

PREVIEW/USE TEXT FEATURES Have students preview the book by looking at the illustrations. Encourage students to use the illustrations to predict the story line. Point out the way in which the text on page 20 is set off with a heading and includes a photo rather than a drawing. Ask: Why might the author have done this?

READ THE BOOK

SET PURPOSE Have children set a purpose for reading *Mr. Post's Class*. They might be interested in the type of teacher Mr. Post will be or what kinds of students will be in his class. After looking at the illustrations, you might guide students to set a purpose related to learning more about volunteering or how to organize a volunteer project.

STRATEGY SUPPORT: PRIOR KNOWLDEGE Encourage students to discuss any prior experience in organizing an activity. Remind students that their prior knowledge will help them understand the story. Their prior experience as volunteers or working on simple fundraising projects might well help them understand some of the issues involved with organizing a volunteer project that involves an entire class.

COMPREHENSION QUESTIONS

PAGE 5 Why were students curious about Mr. Post? *(It was his first year at the school.)*

PAGE 10 What ideas did Mr. Post's students have for volunteer projects? *(recycling, delivering groceries for the elderly; raking leaves for people who couldn't rake)*

PAGE 13 How was the class project organized? *(On sign-up sheets, students volunteered to do things they had time for and liked to do.)*

PAGES 16–17 What do the photos show? How realistic are they? *(They show the students doing volunteer activities. They are very realistic.)*

PAGE 20 How do non-profit groups help with community projects to build homes? *(They pay for materials, equipment, and land, and they organize workers.)*

REVISIT THE BOOK

READER RESPONSE

1. It is a realistic story. The events could happen in real life.
2. Possible responses should demonstrate an understanding of or questions about volunteering.
3. Possible responses: The baseball player showed dedication when he overcame his injury. A dedication was made to the soldiers who served in the war.
4. Possible response: Yes, because I would like to help people in my community.

EXTEND UNDERSTANDING Remind students that *characters* are the people or animals in stories. Since this book focuses largely on the character of Mr. Post, invite students to discuss him. Ask: What kind of person is Mr. Post? How do you know? Would you like Mr. Post to be your teacher? Ask students to describe how they have reached their conclusions about Mr. Post.

RESPONSE OPTIONS

WRITING Invite students to examine the illustrations in the book closely. Assign each illustration to a small group of students, and have each group write a caption that describes what is happening in the picture. Encourage students to write lively captions or dialogue.

WORD WORK Have each student write a story about an imaginary school volunteer project. Each story should include at least six of the vocabulary words.

SOCIAL STUDIES CONNECTION

Time For SOCIAL STUDIES

As a group, have students plan a classroom volunteer project. On the board, write down the steps that students feel must be done to complete the project, from start to finish. Students should consider the needs of the community, interests and skills of students, fundraising, publicity opportunities, and how to celebrate the project's success.

Skill Work

TEACH/REVIEW VOCABULARY

Read aloud the vocabulary words. Ask students to explain words they already know and to look up words they don't know. Have students practice using unfamiliar words in read-aloud sentences.

TARGET SKILL AND STRATEGY

REALISM AND FANTASY Tell students that a *realistic story* tells about something that could happen, while a *fantasy* is a story about something that could not happen. Ask students to point out specific elements of *Mr. Post's Class* that give clues as to which type of story it is. Encourage students to note that many of the illustrations depict activities that could really happen, such as a teacher introducing himself to a class, a boy raking leaves, and girls chatting on the telephone.

PRIOR KNOWLEDGE Tell students that *prior knowledge* is what they know about a given topic, and it comes from their reading and personal experiences. Explain how connecting prior knowledge to a text can help students understand what they read. Read aloud sections of the story, and pause to ask students what it reminds them of. Tell students that they can use their prior knowledge, as well as illustrations, to determine whether a story is a realistic story or a fantasy.

ADDITIONAL SKILL INSTRUCTION

THEME Explain to students that every story has one "big idea" called the *theme*. Instruct students that they can often determine the theme by asking themselves as they read, "What does the writer want me to learn from reading this story?" Tell students that sometimes the theme will be directly stated. Other times, students can look at the actions taken by characters in the story to figure out the theme. Encourage students to think about what the big idea might be as they read *Mr. Post's Class*.

Realism and Fantasy

- A **realistic story** tells about something that could happen.
- A **fantasy** is a story about something that could not happen.

Directions Read the following passage. Then answer the questions below.

Mr. Post explained to the class that he spent the summer working on a volunteer project. He asked the class if they would like to organize a volunteer project to complete during the school year. All the students had suggestions to offer. Someone mentioned that the class could start a recycling program to reduce waste. Another pointed out that students could help the elderly bring their groceries home. Another suggested raking leaves for people. Parents also were excited about the project and wanted to pitch in.

1. Is this paragraph realism or fantasy?

_____

2. Explain your decision in Question 1.

_____

_____

3. What is one realistic idea proposed by the students?

_____

4. Is it realistic for parents to want to help? Why or why not?

_____

_____

5. Write a new first sentence that would make this paragraph seem like a fantasy.

_____

_____

_____

Vocabulary

Directions Choose the word from the box that best completes each sentence.
Write the word on the line.

> ## Check the Words You Know
>
> ___ community   ___ enthusiasm   ___ labor   ___ mural
> ___ nonprofit   ___ organization   ___ reporter   ___ sign-up
> ___ success   ___ volunteer

1. The volunteer _____ helped students plan and buy supplies.

2. The students were so excited, they could not contain their _____ .

3. A _____ gives his or her time to help others.

4. A newspaper _____ visited the surprised students.

5. Many people from the _____ had project ideas for the students.

6. Raking leaves required the students to perform physical _____ .

7. The students made a big _____ to hang on the wall.

8. A _____ organization does not make a profit.

9. Mr. Post hung a _____ sheet on the door so students could volunteer.

10. The community project to clean the park was a huge _____ .

Directions Use the sentence you wrote on page 14 and write a paragraph about
volunteering, using as many vocabulary words as you can. Your paragraph should
be fantasy.

_____

_____

_____

_____

_____

© Pearson Education 3

What's Money All About?

SUMMARY This book gives a lively historical perspective on how and why we began using money. It explains the origins of trading, buying, bargaining, and selling.

LESSON VOCABULARY

bargaining	compromise
currency	mints
wampum	

INTRODUCE THE BOOK

INTRODUCE THE TITLE AND AUTHOR Discuss with students the title and the author of *What's Money All About?* Based on the title and the cover illustrations, ask students to describe what they imagine this book will be about. Ask students if they can identify any of the kinds of money on the cover.

BUILD BACKGROUND Ask students to discuss how they get money for the things they want and how they use their money once they have it. Discuss the different kinds of money, such as coins, bills, and checks. Ask students which kind of money is easier for them to handle, which kind is safest, and which kind is more valuable to them.

PREVIEW/USE TEXT FEATURES Have students look at the chapter headings and the illustrations and discuss how these text elements help organize the information in the book. Ask students how the chapter headings help them predict what this book is about.

READ THE BOOK

SET PURPOSE Have students set a purpose for reading *What's Money All About?* Students' curiosity about how money came about or their interest in having their own money should guide this purpose. If students are interested, suggest that they later do research on the different kinds of money in the world.

STRATEGY SUPPORT: SUMMARIZE As students read about bartering and how our system of money began, prompt them to summarize. Summarizing will help students zero in on the most important points in the book. Suggest that students take notes as they read the story, writing down what they consider to be the key points.

COMPREHENSION QUESTIONS

PAGE 7 What is the major problem that arises when people barter? *(Sometimes people cannot agree on the value of goods.)*

PAGE 13 What is the benefit of a coin-based system of money? *(Coins are small and easy to carry.)*

PAGE 15 What was the sequence of events in the development of money during colonial times and the early days of independence? *(Each colony had its own money; the country needed its own money; Congress began making money so the states could trade with each other more easily.)*

PAGE 16 How many mints are in the United States? *(four)*

Fiction or nonfiction book?
How do you know

REVISIT THE BOOK

READER RESPONSE

1. Traveling traders call out to local traders; traveling traders leave their goods on the beach; local traders leave their goods on the beach; each group returns and decides if the trade is fair; different items are then added or removed to make trade fair.

2. The ancient Egyptians sent stones, copper, grains, and papyrus to ancient Lebanon. In return, they received wood such as fir, cedar, and pine.

3. Possible response: Sometimes two people who are bargaining have to compromise about a price.

4. Possible response: I could see the color and design of the coin.

EXTEND UNDERSTANDING Discuss with students how chapters in books can help organize complicated material. Go over the four chapters with students and discuss what information is in each chapter and why. Ask students how they can tell what each chapter is going to be about and how each chapter is a progression of the last.

RESPONSE OPTIONS

WRITING Have students imagine that for one day no money is available, so people must barter. Ask students to write a paragraph each about what that day would be like.

ELL Have students discuss whether bartering is common in their home country and, if so, whether it is used for certain types of goods and services or as a general practice.

SOCIAL STUDIES CONNECTION

Time For SOCIAL STUDIES

Have students make up a new kind of money. Discuss whether their money will be coins or bills or something altogether different. Ask students how they will determine the value of their money and what it should look like. Once students have decided these things, ask them to make a grocery list showing what bread, milk, and fruit might cost with this new money.

Skill Work

TEACH/REVIEW VOCABULARY

Tell students you have chosen a word from the list of vocabulary words. It is their job to guess what the word is, based on clues you give. For example, "What word has three words in it?" *(bargaining, which has* bar, gain, *and* bargain *in it)*

TARGET SKILL AND STRATEGY

SEQUENCE Remind students that the *sequence* in a story is the order in which events occur. To illustrate, ask students to write a short paragraph about how to get from home to school, keeping the steps in sequence. Have students read their sequences to the class.

SUMMARIZE Remind students that *summarizing* means boiling down the main idea of a story or text into a sentence or two. In order to do this, students must identify the most important ideas or events. Ask students to summarize their last vacation or what they did over the weekend.

ADDITIONAL SKILL INSTRUCTION

DRAW CONCLUSIONS Remind students that *drawing conclusions* means to think about the facts and details that are presented and, sometimes with the benefit of personal experience, to decide something about them. By drawing conclusions, students can enhance their understanding of the text. Encourage students to draw conclusions as they read.

Sequence

- The **sequence** of events in a stor____ ____ order in which the events occur.

Directions Answer t___ _____ ___s below.

1. What is the se_____ _____ n in bartering?

_____

_____

2. What was the sequence of events in the trade between the Egyptians and the Lebanese?

_____

_____

_____

3. What happens during a silent trade? Summarize the steps.

_____

_____

_____

4. Trace the steps from bartering to the invention of coin money.

_____

_____

_____

5. Summarize why salt eventually was no longer used for money.

_____

_____

_____

Vocabulary

Directions Write the words from the box in the proper boxes. Note: There are three words that can go in both boxes.

Check the Words You Know

___bargaining   ___compromise   ___currency
___mints   ___wampum

Nouns	Verbs

Directions Draw a line from the vocabulary word to its correct definition.

1. bargaining
2. compromise
3. currency
4. mints
5. wampum

a. to give up some of your demands to reach an agreement
b. money
c. beads made from shells
d. places where money is made
e. when two people work together to come up with an agreement

Maggie McGee and Me at the Mint

SUMMARY Chris Chen and his friend Maggie McGee have a job to do in this fictional tale: They want to be the first students on their class field trip to answer ten questions about the U.S. mint. The sequence of events leads them on an interesting journey behind the scenes of America's coin maker.

LESSON VOCABULARY

brainstormed	detectors
engrave	grooves
precious	recited
replicas	

INTRODUCE THE BOOK

INTRODUCE THE TITLE AND AUTHOR Discuss with students the title and the author of *Maggie McGee and Me at the Mint*. Ask if any students collect coins. If so, what kinds of coins do they collect? Ask students what they know about the U.S. mint.

BUILD BACKGROUND Discuss with students what they know about U.S. coins. Talk about subjects such as what the coins are made of, their denominations, and the different pictures on them.

PREVIEW/USE ILLUSTRATIONS Point out that the genre of the book is fiction. Then have students look through the illustrations in the book. Discuss with students what they can tell about the boy and girl in the pictures and what they think the two are doing.

READ THE BOOK

SET PURPOSE Based on the genre and title of the book, have students tell why they would like to read it. Remind students that they may have more than one reason for wanting to read a book.

STRATEGY SUPPORT: VISUALIZE Read with students question 1 in the Reader Response section of the book. To help students visualize the order of events in the story, have them jot down notes about the order in which Chris and Maggie answer the questions.

ELL Have students use a sequence of events flow chart (see page 138) to complete the Strategy Support activity above. To check their understanding of the text, have pairs of students exchange charts when they have finished reading.

COMPREHENSION QUESTIONS

PAGE 4 What sequence of events leads to Chris and Maggie's becoming friends? *(Johnnie Jaspers had been bothering Chris; Maggie beats Johnnie in the battle of the minds; Johnnie stops bothering Chris; Maggie tells Chris to stick with her.)*

PAGE 5 On this page, Chris starts to tell the story of the class trip to the mint. When did the trip take place—before, during, or after Chris tells the story? *(Before—he is telling about something that happened in the past.)*

PAGE 6 How did the contest at the mint get started? *(Maggie suggested it, and Ms. Chesterfield agreed to it.)*

PAGE 12 What words does the author use to help you visualize the original image of the eagle on American coins? *(pigeon, laughed, majestic bird of prey)*

REVISIT THE BOOK

READER RESPONSE

1. 1, 4, 5, 9, 8, 10, 2, 3, 6, 7
2. Possible response: sharp corners, dozens of tiny windows, bright white walls; responses will vary.
3. Possible responses: exhibit: things shown together in a museum; a display or presentation. Other answers should include appropriate words, use context clues correctly, and contain dictionary definitions.
4. Possible response: When was the Philadelphia mint built?

EXTEND UNDERSTANDING Point out to students that sometimes the author changes the setting within a story. Have students reread the first three pages of the book. Ask: What clue words does the author use to tell the reader the time and place of the story? *(Possible responses: outside the United States mint, after we won the class contest, on the day she challenged and beat the bully, afterwards).* Does the setting change in these pages? What makes you think this? *(Yes; Chris starts his story in the present at an unknown place, then he shifts to the day Maggie beat Johnnie in the battle of the minds, then he shifts again to the day of the class trip to the mint.)*

RESPONSE OPTIONS

WRITING Have students work in pairs to write short stories about other, new adventures with Chris and Maggie. Tell students to write the events in sequence, so that there is a time order to what happens.

SOCIAL STUDIES CONNECTION

Provide students with information about how coins are made by the mint. Have groups create diagrams showing the stages in the minting process and then share their drawings with the class.

Skill Work

TEACH/REVIEW VOCABULARY

Write a matching activity on the board with the vocabulary words in one column and the definitions in another. Direct students to the locations of the words in the book and have them try to match each word to its correct definition using context clues.

TARGET SKILL AND STRATEGY

SEQUENCE Review with students that a *sequence* is the order in which events occur. Remind them that, in a story, events are sometimes told out of their proper sequence. Sometimes the sequence of events may be interrupted to tell about events that happened earlier. Tell students to stop and reread parts of the story if they are not sure they are following the sequence of events correctly.

VISUALIZE Remind students that to *visualize* means to create pictures in their minds as they read. Visualizing may also help them better follow the sequence of events in a story. Suggest that as they read, students create mental pictures of the events.

ADDITIONAL SKILL INSTRUCTION

SETTING Review with students that *setting* is the time and place in which events occur in a story. Have students point out the most likely place setting for the selection—the mint. Invite students to guess when the events take place, either with a specific or general time. Remind them that an author may not state an exact time and place. Tell students to look for clues to the time and place of the action in the story as they read.

Sequence

- **Sequence** is the order in which things happen in a story—what happens first, next, and last.

Directions Read the following passage. Then list the sequence of events that leads to Sam and Nathan's buying their video game.

My name is Sam, which is short for Samantha. I want to tell you about a time my friend Nathan and I outsmarted our own parents. We didn't do anything wrong. We just proved that we were more creative than they thought we were.

Let me start from the beginning. Nathan and I wanted to buy a video game together. We had a great plan. We would take turns keeping the game at each other's houses. The problem was that our parents did not want us to have the game. They thought it was too expensive and that we would fight over it. So they made us a deal. They said if we could save the money ourselves, then we could buy it.

I think my parents thought they were being tricky. They know I am not a good saver. Once when I wanted a dress they didn't like, they made me save for it. The store stopped selling the dress by the time I had enough money to buy it. My parents were hoping the same thing would happen with the video game.

But Nathan and I knew we had to act quickly. Instead of saving money, we opened a lemonade stand. It was so hot that summer, people came to the stand by the dozens! Within two weeks we had enough money for the game. Now we play it all the time. And our parents have to admit we're two pretty smart friends!

First, _____

_____

Next, _____

_____

Next, _____

_____

Then, _____

_____

Finally, _____

_____

Vocabulary

Directions Choose the word from the box that best matches each definition. Write the word on the line.

Check the Words You Know

___brainstormed   ___detectors   ___engrave   ___grooves

___precious   ___recited   ___replicas
---

1. _____ to cut deeply into

2. _____ copies of original pieces of art or other objects

3. _____ long, narrow channels cut with tools

4. _____ repeated or said aloud from memory

5. _____ costly; valuable

Directions Choose all the words from the box that fit each category. Write the words on the lines.

6. Verbs _____

7. Nouns _____

8. Plural Words _____

Directions Write a news article on the lines. Use as many of the vocabulary words as you can.

_____

_____

_____

_____

_____

_____

Mr. Grim and the Goose That Laid Golden Eggs

SUMMARY This is a fantasy that offers a real message about money. The book retells the famous fable about a goose that lays golden eggs with a modern and practical spin about the importance of investing. It supports the lesson concept of how money can be earned, saved, and invested.

LESSON VOCABULARY

deposit	gleamed
glittering	invest
mortgage	stockbroker

INTRODUCE THE BOOK

INTRODUCE THE TITLE AND AUTHOR Discuss with students the title and the author of *Mr. Grim and The Goose That Laid Golden Eggs*. Direct students to look at the cover illustration to see if they can gain clues to what the story might be about. Ask students to identify what elements in the illustration look realistic and which appear to be fantasy.

BUILD BACKGROUND Ask students if they have ever received large sums of money and, if so, whether they spent it, saved it, or had their parents invest it for them. Discuss with students the different ways they can handle, save, or spend money.

PREVIEW/USE ILLUSTRATIONS As students preview the book, the amusing illustrations of the goose and the grumpy Mr. Grim will probably attract their interest. Suggest that they notice how Mr. Grim's expression hardly changes in the illustrations, but the goose's expression does. Explain that this may give them clues as to whose character changes in the story and whose character does not. Ask students to predict, based on the illustrations, which character ends up getting what he or she wants.

READ THE BOOK

SET PURPOSE Have students set a purpose for reading *Mr. Grim and The Goose That Laid Golden Eggs*. Students' interest in earning and saving money, as well as their interest in fables, should guide this purpose. Suggest that students think about how we learn about ourselves by reading stories about animals.

STRATEGY SUPPORT: MONITOR AND FIX UP Discuss with students that it is important to monitor, or keep an eye on, their understanding of what they are reading. Remind them that there are different ways to fix up a comprehension problem. Suggest that students write notes about what is happening in the story. They can track the story and can check their notes if the story stops making sense. Also tell students that if they are asked a question about the story, they can reread to review information they may have forgotten.

COMPREHENSION QUESTIONS

PAGE 4 What is the first detail in the story that gives you a clue that this story is a fantasy and not a realistic story? *(The goose knocks on the door.)*

PAGE 13 What does the goose think would be a wise thing for Mr. Grim to do? *(She wants him to stop wasting his money trying to get more eggs and to invest the money he already has.)*

PAGE 19 Does Mr. Grim's character change at the end of the story? *(No, he is the same as he has always been. He did not learn any lesson and he still wants more than what he has.)*

REVISIT THE BOOK

READER RESPONSE

1. Possible responses: It's a fantasy because of the talking goose, the golden eggs, the talking dog, and the goose's buying land.
2. food, spray of water, scary costume, house, and dog
3. Possible response: a way to pay for a house over time; My parents have a mortgage for our house.
4. Possible responses: Yes; Appreciate what you have; don't be greedy; invest your money wisely and patiently; save your money, and it will grow.

EXTEND UNDERSTANDING As students read the story, remind them that stories that teach a lesson and feature talking animals are called *fables*. Discuss with students what the lesson of this fable might be and how they can apply that lesson to their own lives.

RESPONSE OPTIONS

WRITING Suggest that students consider why Mr. Grim behaves as he does in the story. Ask them to imagine that they are Mr. Grim and suggest they write a letter to the goose, asking for a second chance.

SOCIAL STUDIES CONNECTION

Time For SOCIAL STUDIES

Students can learn more about money by starting a class bank. Suggest that each student put a dime into the class bank every week. Invite students to keep track of the money in a class bankbook. After a number of weeks, count the money. Students should then decide whether to save more money, to spend some of the money, or to spend all of the money.

Skill Work

TEACH/REVIEW VOCABULARY

Reinforce the meanings of the vocabulary words by having students free-associate other words about money, saving, or spending that they may know.

ELL Suggest that students take a word, such as *deposit,* and generate more words that relate to this activity. They can record their words in a web.

TARGET SKILL AND STRATEGY

REALISM AND FANTASY Remind students that a *realistic story* deals with things that can happen, and a *fantasy* deals with things that could not happen. As students read the book, ask them to write down story details that indicate that this is a fantasy. Students may also jot down details that seem realistic.

MONITOR AND FIX UP Remind students that *monitoring* their reading means keeping track of what parts of the story they don't understand. *Fix up* refers to how they can improve their understanding by doing things like taking notes, reading on, and rereading. Tell students that if they monitor and fix up as they read, it will be easier to keep track of the realistic or fantastic details.

ADDITIONAL SKILL INSTRUCTION

CHARACTER Remind students that *characters* are the people or animals in a story who do the action. Every character has traits, which are the things we know about the character that can help us predict how the character will act in the story. Have students create a character chart for both Mr. Grim and the goose. As they read, ask students to fill in the chart with the traits of both characters.

Realism and Fantasy

- A **realistic story** tells about something that could happen.
- A **fantasy** is a story about something that could not happen.

1. What are some of the realistic things in this story?

_____

_____

_____

2. What is realistic about using gold to buy things in the story?
   What is fantasy?

_____

_____

_____

3. What is a lesson or moral that you learned from this story?

_____

_____

_____

4. What things about the goose are realistic? What things are not realistic?

_____

_____

_____

Directions Write two statements about money that are realistic and two statements that are fantasy.

5. _____

_____

6. _____

_____

7. _____

_____

8. _____

_____

Vocabulary

Directions Write the correct vocabulary words in the blanks below.

Check the Words You Know

___deposit	___gleamed	___glittering
___invest	___mortgage	___stockbroker

Sally really wanted to buy her own planet, but she knew it would cost a lot. She decided to do some chores to earn money. First she polished her mother's beautiful silver tray until it **(1)** _____.

Then she washed the dishes. When she had put away the last clean,

(2) _____ glass, her mother paid Sally five dollars.

Sally thought about using the money to make a **(3)** _____

in the bank. Instead, she decided to **(4)** _____ the

money in the stock market, so she called a **(5)** _____.

Sally thinks that in a few years she will be able to take out a

(6) _____ on a planet or pay for it over time.

Directions Select three vocabulary words and use each in a sentence.

_____

_____

_____

_____

_____

_____

_____

Pizza with a Twist

SUMMARY This is a fantasy about how a group of children learns about different cultures when they magically travel around the world to buy ingredients for a popular meal—pizza. This story also shows how different people can have things in common.

LESSON VOCABULARY

awnings	bazaar
confused	garlic
ingredients	oregano
vendors	

INTRODUCE THE BOOK

INTRODUCE THE TITLE AND AUTHOR Discuss with students the title and the author of *Pizza with a Twist*. Based on the cover and the title, have students speculate what this book will be about.

BUILD BACKGROUND Discuss with students what it means to give something a "twist." Make sure students understand how the figurative meaning of *twist* is related to its literal meaning. Ask: What kinds of things can you twist literally (for real)? What kinds of things can you twist figuratively (in a manner of speaking)? Explain that many foods that we eat in the United States originated in other countries, and invite students to compare and contrast how their family's version of a common meal like pasta might differ from someone else's. How might different spices or ingredients add a "twist" to the meal?

PREVIEW/USE ILLUSTRATIONS Invite students to look at the illustrations and see if they can gain clues as to what this story might be about and where it might take place. Ask students what details help them with their answers.

READ THE BOOK

SET PURPOSE Have students set a purpose for reading *Pizza with a Twist*. Students' interest in pizza and their natural curiosity about what the "twist" in the story might be should guide this purpose. Suggest that students think about how changing, or "twisting," things can make them more interesting.

STRATEGY SUPPORT: STORY STRUCTURE As students read the story, suggest that they make notes about the sequence of events in the story. Ask them to consider whether any of the events could happen in any other order and how that might change the story.

COMPREHENSION QUESTIONS

PAGES 4, 12, 15 List some of the different settings of this book. *(Possible responses: a Russian street, a Greek market, Jake's house)*

PAGES 8–9 Do you think Bo, Ruby, and Jake have a good time on their journey through different cultures? Why do you think so? *(Possible response: Bo says he is really enjoying the trip; characters are smiling in the illustrations.)*

PAGE 15 Why do Bo, Ruby, and Jake cross items off their list? *(to make sure they have everything they need)*

PAGES 18–19 Write out the way Bo, Ruby, and Jake make pizza. Use the text structure of a recipe. *(Prepare pizza dough in the pan. Grate Parmesan cheese and slice mozzarella. For the sauce, chop tomatoes, basil, oregano, and garlic and cook them in a pan. Separately slice olives and pineapple. Spoon sauce over pizza dough, add the two cheeses, and arrange olives and pineapples on top. Place in oven and bake until done. Take out of oven, using mitts. Allow to cool slightly before cutting.)*

REVISIT THE BOOK

READER RESPONSE

1. Possible response: curious, adventurous, and responsible
2. Peru—tomatoes; Italy—cheeses; India—basil; Russia—garlic; Greece—oregano and olives; Brazil—pineapple
3. *Unwrapped* means "removed the covering."
4. Possible response: I would visit Italy because I love Italian food.

EXTEND UNDERSTANDING Remind students that fantasy is an element in a story that isn't real. Discuss with students what elements of *Pizza with a Twist* are fantasy and why. Ask students how the addition of fantasy added to their enjoyment of the story and what information they learned through the fantasy that they wouldn't have learned otherwise.

RESPONSE OPTIONS

WRITING Suggest that students write about the places they would visit if they could snap their fingers the same way Jake does. Direct students to provide lots of sensory details to set their scenes.

SOCIAL STUDIES CONNECTION

Time For
SOCIAL STUDIES

Suggest that students think of their favorite food, such as pasta or Chinese noodles, and research the country where the food originated. Direct students to write a few sentences about their findings.

Skill Work

TEACH/REVIEW VOCABULARY

Review the vocabulary words. Discuss how the word *confused* has a suffix, *–ed*, that changes the meaning of the word. Ask students how the other vocabulary words can change their meanings by adding or removing suffixes and prefixes or by making them plural or singular.

ELL Have students write the definitions of the vocabulary words and use each word in a sentence.

TARGET SKILL AND STRATEGY

CHARACTER AND SETTING Remind students that a *character* is a person or animal in a story, and the *setting* is where the story takes place. Ask students to think of themselves as characters and to write down ten words that describe what kind of characters they are. Have them write ten words that describe where they live, as if their homes were settings. Encourage them to use sensory words.

STORY STRUCTURE Remind students that *story structure* is how a story is organized, with one event leading to another. To illustrate story structure, go through the book with the students and point out two events that are related. Then have students work in pairs to find other examples of related events.

ADDITIONAL SKILL INSTRUCTION

SEQUENCE Remind students that *sequence* is the order in which things happen. Suggest that as they read the story, students pay attention to how events happen. Give students a story outline in which the beginning, middle, and end are out of order, and invite them to restructure it.

Character and Setting

- **Characters** are the people or animals who do the action in a story.
- The **setting** is where the story takes place.

Directions To better understand *Pizza with a Twist,* answer the questions below.

1. First, name all the characters and write one detail about each.

_____

_____

_____

2. Now name settings in the story and write one detail about each.

_____

_____

_____

_____

3. Write a detail that tells what one of the places smells like.

_____

_____

4. Write a detail that tells what one of the places looks like.

_____

_____

5. Write a detail that tells what one of the places sounds like.

_____

_____

Name _____

Vocabulary

Directions Fill in the crossword puzzle by using the correct vocabulary word for each clue.

Check the Words You Know

___awnings   ___bazaar   ___confused   ___garlic
___ingredients   ___oregano   ___vendors

ACROSS

2. a strong-smelling bulb used as seasoning
6. pieces of cloth stretched out to shade people from the sun
7. people who sell things in an open market

DOWN

1. parts that make up a recipe
3. not sure what is going on
4. a tasty herb used in pizza sauce and other Italian dishes
5. an open market in India

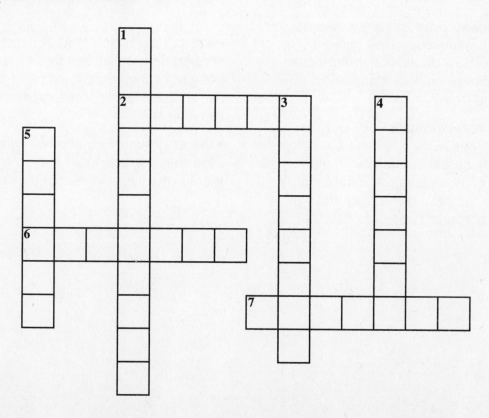

© Pearson Education 3

Penguins On Parade

SUMMARY Though Antarctica's emperor penguins are perhaps the best known birds of their kind, there are many other varieties of penguins that are just as interesting. The book describes how these birds are equipped to thrive in some of the coldest and most isolated places on Earth.

LESSON VOCABULARY

blubber	brood patch
crest	down
incubate	molt
rookery	

INTRODUCE THE BOOK

INTRODUCE THE TITLE AND AUTHOR Discuss with students the title and the author of *Penguins On Parade*. Ask them to look at the cover photo and describe what it tells about penguins. Based on their responses, talk about what information they think the author will provide in this book.

BUILD BACKGROUND Have students discuss what comes to mind when they think of penguins. Ask: How do penguins differ from other birds? Where do your ideas about penguins come from?

PREVIEW/USE TEXT FEATURES Point out the sidebars on pages 4, 5, 7, 9, and 13. Ask: What kinds of information can be found in these features? How does the information in each relate to the rest of the text, and why might the author have chosen to use them?

READ THE BOOK

SET PURPOSE Have students set a purpose for reading *Penguins On Parade*. They should be guided by their impressions from skimming the heads, photos, captions, and sidebars.

STRATEGY SUPPORT: GRAPHIC ORGANIZERS Tell students that different graphic organizers are suited for different purposes. Webs and charts can help readers determine cause and effect, compare and contrast story elements, keep track of vocabulary, and perform other functions. Introduce students to a variety of organizers for a variety of purposes and encourage their use during reading.

COMPREHENSION QUESTIONS

PAGE 3 All penguins live in what part of the world? *(the Southern Hemisphere)*

PAGES 6–8 What is the topic of this section? What is the main idea of this section? *(emperor penguins; how they incubate their eggs)*

PAGE 11 How is an emperor penguin's beak shaped differently than that of an adelie penguin? *(Emperor's is long and thin to catch fish and adelie's is short and stubby for catching krill.)*

PAGE 17 Different varieties of penguins share lives that are tied to what type of environment? *(the sea and its marine life)*

REVIST THE BOOK

READER RESPONSE

1. Possible response: There are many different varieties of penguins in the world, and they all have ways to survive in cold weather.
2. Possible response: Emperor Penguins— world's largest penguins, live in Antarctica; Little Blue Penguins—world's smallest penguins, live in Australia, New Zealand, and Tasmania; Both—cannot fly, have dark feathers on their backs and white feathers on their bellies
3. Sentences will vary.
4. calcium

EXTEND UNDERSTANDING Direct students to page 3. Ask: How does the map differ from most other maps you have seen? What continents are shown and where? Students may use a globe or atlas to help them find answers.

RESPONSE OPTIONS

WRITING Ask: How do people stay warm when they are outdoors in cold weather? How are these ways similar to or different from those of penguins? Have students answer these questions in one or two paragraphs.

ELL On the board, write simple sentences that students can complete by writing a word or two, for example: *Penguins have a layer of _____ that stores energy and blocks out cold.*

WORD WORK Help students sort words related to aspects of penguins' lives into categories such as *body features, food,* and *dwellings.*

SCIENCE CONNECTION

Remind students that penguins have special characteristics that enable them to survive in specific types of environments. Discuss how other animals have characteristics that make them well-suited for where they live.

Skill Work

TEACH/REVIEW VOCABULARY

Have students look at the glossary. Ask volunteers to point out familiar terms and explain what they mean.

TARGET SKILL AND STRATEGY

MAIN IDEA The *main idea* is the most important idea about the topic. To find it, students must determine the relative importance of information they read. *Supporting details* are pieces of information that tell more about the main idea. Model how to ask questions to find the main idea of a book. Ask: In a word or two, what is this book about? (This identifies the topic.) What is the most important idea about the topic? (This identifies the main idea.) What are some details that tell more about the main idea? Tell students to identify the main idea of the book as they read.

GRAPHIC ORGANIZERS *Graphic organizers* are pictorial devices that help students view and construct relationships among concepts, such as identifying main idea and supporting details or determining causes and effects. Before reading, create a *KWL* (*K*now, *W*ant to know, *L*earned) chart on the board about penguins. Ask students to share what they already know about these birds and to identify what they would like to know about them. During their reading, have students look for answers to their questions. Record all responses in the appropriate columns.

ADDITIONAL SKILL INSTRUCTION

COMPARE AND CONTRAST Tell students that to *compare* is to identify how two or more things are alike and to *contrast* is to identify how they are different. Ask students to use graphic organizers to compare and contrast aspects of different penguins in the book, such as their natural habitats.

Main Idea

- The **main idea** is the most important idea about a paragraph, passage, or story.
- **Supporting details** are pieces of information that tell more about the main idea.

Directions Read each passage. Then answer the questions that follow.

The Southern Hemisphere is the natural home to the world's penguins. Penguins live on the Galápagos Islands and in Australia, New Zealand, Africa, South America, and the islands that surround Antarctica. They also live on Antarctica itself. All penguins share lives that are tied to the sea and the Southern Hemisphere's marine ecosystems.

1. In a few words, what is this paragraph about?

_____

2. What is the main idea of the paragraph?

_____

3. What is an important detail that tells more about the main idea?

_____

_____

Emperor penguins reduce heat loss through their feet by standing on their heels. This keeps the rest of the foot from touching cold ice.

Male emperor penguins also huddle to help conserve heat. The temperature in the middle of an emperor penguin huddle can be 95°F! Of course, some penguins must stand on the outside of the huddle. So what do they do to stay warm? They rotate. The penguins on the outside gradually push their way into the middle of the huddle. This way, each penguin gets a chance to become warmed.

4. What is the main idea of the passage?

_____

5. What is one detail that tells more about the main idea?

_____

Vocabulary

Directions Choose the word from the box that best completes each sentence. Write the word on the line.

Check the Words You Know

___blubber   ___brood patch   ___crest   ___down
___incubate   ___molt   ___rookery

---

1. Emperor penguins choose to _____ their eggs during the winter.

2. Large groups of penguins gather in a _____ to raise their young.

3. A penguin's _____ stores energy and helps protect the penguin from cold weather.

4. Fluffy inner feathers known as _____ trap air to keep penguins warm.

5. Penguins _____ when their old feathers get worn out.

6. Male penguins have a featherless area of skin known as a

   _____, which warms their eggs.

7. Some penguins have a _____ that sticks up from their heads.

Directions Use the context clues in the above sentences to define these words.

8. molt _____

_____

9. rookery _____

_____

10. blubber _____

_____

The Song Makers Go to Salem

SUMMARY Tabitha struggles with her conscience after witnessing her friend Abbey steal money from a school fund-raising drive. Unsure of whether or not to tell on her friend, Tabitha finally confronts Abbey, discovers the reason behind the theft, and works out a constructive solution where Abbey takes responsibility for what she did.

LESSON VOCABULARY

anxious	concentrate
erupted	frantically
relieved	solution
suspect	

INTRODUCE THE BOOK

INTRODUCE THE TITLE AND AUTHOR Discuss with students the title and the author of *The Song Makers Go to Salem.* Who might the Song Makers be? What might they do? Why might they want to go to a place called Salem?

BUILD BACKGROUND Have students discuss real-life conflicts where they or someone they know struggled to make the right decision in an uncertain situation. What made the decision so difficult?

PREVIEW/USE ILLUSTRATIONS Have students look at the illustrations. Ask them to focus on the characters' poses and facial expressions and to discuss what they think the characters are doing and feeling in these pictures.

READ THE BOOK

SET PURPOSE Have students set a purpose for reading *The Song Makers Go to Salem.* Encourage them to focus on how the characters are reaching their goal of raising enough money for their trip to Salem. Students' own experiences in setting and reaching goals should guide this purpose.

STRATEGY SUPPORT: VISUALIZE Ask students to practice visualizing specific scenes and events while reading. Tell them to identify words and phrases from the text that helped them form mental pictures. Remind them that these words and phrases can involve any of the senses. Then have students draw pictures or act out skits based on their visualizations.

COMPREHENSION QUESTIONS

PAGE 3 Why is Tabitha's school chorus raising money? (*They will travel to Salem for their spring performance.*)

PAGE 12 Why did Abbey take the money from the chorus's money box? (*She needed it to pay for a chorus shirt. Her family did not have the money because her father lost his job.*)

PAGE 12 What did Abbey's confession tell you about her character? (*Possible responses: Abbey can make wrong decisions, but she is not greedy.*)

PAGE 20 What might Tabitha have done if Abbey refused to admit her mistake? (*Possible responses: Tabitha might have told on her. Tabitha might not trust Abbey again.*)

REVISIT THE BOOK

READER RESPONSE

1. Possible response: She is a thoughtful and honest person.
2. Possible response: "Tears were running down Abbey's cheeks, but she had a big smile on her face, too."
3. Possible response: simple or clear
4. Responses will vary.

EXTEND UNDERSTANDING Explore the use of theme. Tell students to ask themselves questions such as, "What does the author want me to learn from reading this story?" Then have them determine the story's "big idea" and explain how the events and characters support their findings.

RESPONSE OPTIONS

WRITING Ask students to write a letter to either Tabitha or Abbey with comments on their actions and advice on how to make good choices in the future.

WORD WORK Challenge students to write or verbalize sentences that incorporate two or more vocabulary words. Provide an example: "I couldn't *concentrate* because I felt *anxious.*"

SOCIAL STUDIES CONNECTION

Time For SOCIAL STUDIES

Discuss recent or historic events where people struggled to do the right thing in the midst of uncertainty and hardship. What factors made their decisions so difficult? How did their choices change your community or the world?

Skill Work

TEACH/REVIEW VOCABULARY

Ask students to decipher the contextual meaning of each vocabulary word by reading the sentences that precede and follow the sentence in which the word appears.

TARGET SKILL AND STRATEGY

CHARACTER A *character* is a person who takes part in the events of a story. C*haracter traits* are qualities that usually relate to the character's personality. Have students analyze the character traits of Tabitha and Abbey while they are reading. How are they alike? How are they different? Students should support their statements with clues and details. Then have them make predictions about what Tabitha and Abbey might do after the story ends.

ELL Ask students simple questions about the characters, plot, or theme.

VISUALIZE Students can enhance their understanding of characters through *visualization.* Invite them to use their own knowledge of people and fictional characters to create mental pictures of Tabitha, Abbey, and other characters. Encourage them to be detailed by asking questions such as, "How did the cookies smell? What did her voice sound like?"

ADDITIONAL SKILL INSTRUCTION

CAUSE AND EFFECT Tell students that an *effect* is something that happens and a *cause* is why that thing happens. Have students practice identifying cause and effect in simple sentences such as, "I am hungry because I skipped breakfast." *(What happened: "I am hungry." Why it happened: "I skipped breakfast.")* Understanding cause and effect can help students better understand the motivations of characters in a book. Ask them to identify cause-and-effect relationships while they are reading.

Name _____

Character

- A **character** is a person who takes part in the events of a story.
- The qualities of a character are known as **character traits** and usually relate to his or her personality.

Directions Fill in the graphic organizers below using details from your reading.

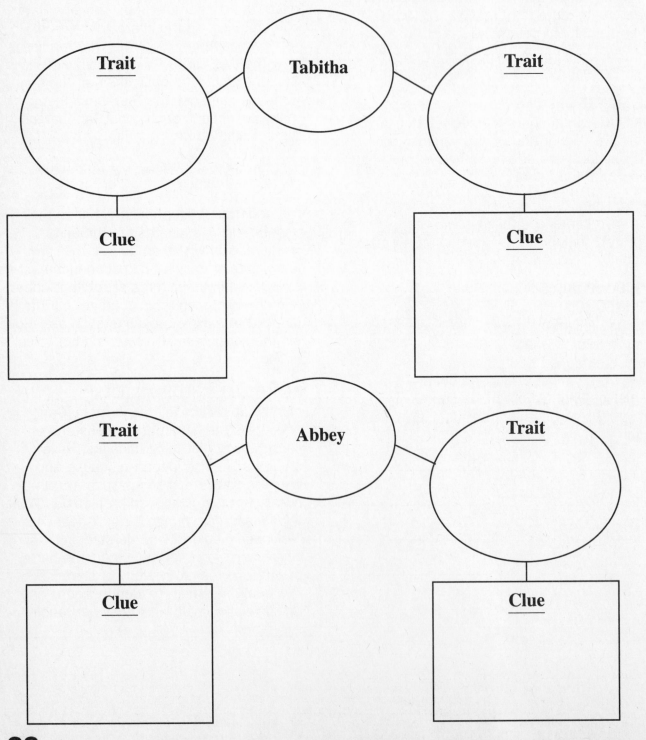

38

Name _____

Vocabulary

Directions Choose the word from the box that best completes each sentence. Write the word on the line.

Check the Words You Know

___anxious   ___concentrate   ___erupted   ___frantically
___relieved   ___solution   ___suspect

---

1. Tabitha fought hard to find a _____ to the problem.

2. Zoe _____ waved her hands at Tabitha.

3. People often _____ too much on what others will think.

4. Tabitha didn't just _____ that Abbey had taken money— she knew it.

5. Tabitha was _____ because she wasn't sure how Abbey would react.

6. Abbey felt _____ after she admitted she had taken the money.

7. The crowd _____ with applause as Abbey arrived with her delicious cookies.

Directions What do you think happened after the story ended? Write a paragraph about the Song Makers' trip to Salem. Use as many vocabulary words as you can.

_____
_____
_____
_____
_____
_____
_____

Collecting Dreams

SUMMARY Tina cannot understand why her mother loves collecting teacups. Tina later discovers the joy of collecting while searching for a birthday gift for her mother and sees her mother's teacups in a whole new light.

LESSON VOCABULARY

collectibles	credit
fond	kaleidoscope
porcelain	propped
rim	specialize
suspiciously	

INTRODUCE THE BOOK

INTRODUCE THE TITLE AND AUTHOR Discuss with students the title and the author of *Collecting Dreams*. Ask: Based on the title, do you think the story will be fiction or nonfiction? Why? Then have them look at the cover illustration and talk about how the title might relate to the picture.

BUILD BACKGROUND Ask students if they collect objects such as dolls or baseball cards. What makes those objects so special? Discuss reasons why people collect things in general.

PREVIEW/USE TEXT FEATURES Have students preview the book by looking at the title and illustrations. What predictions can they make about the story based on these features?

READ THE BOOK

SET PURPOSE Have students set a purpose for reading *Collecting Dreams*. Students' own interest in collecting objects should guide this purpose. Suggest that they think about what collections can reveal about the interests and personalities of collectors.

STRATEGY SUPPORT: MONITOR AND FIX UP
Tell students that they can monitor their comprehension of a story by creating an outline of it. An outline is a plan that shows how a story is organized. Using outlines to determine and keep track of the most important ideas of a book can help students gain comprehension. Invite students to create an outline of *Collecting Dreams* during and after reading.

ELL Use a graphic organizer to show steps in a process. Help students outline the steps that Tina and her father took to find a gift for Tina's mother.

COMPREHENSION QUESTIONS

PAGE 6 Early in the book, how did Tina feel about her mother's collection of teacups? *(Tina pretended to like teacups but did not understand her mother's fascination with them.)*

PAGE 8 How did Tina's father feel about his wife's teacups? *(He supported her hobby as seen in the trip to the collectibles fair.)*

PAGE 23 How did Tina's feelings about her mother's teacups change by the end of the book? *(When Tina bought a collectible kaleidoscope at the fair, she understood why her mother loved collecting pretty objects.)*

REVISIT THE BOOK

READER RESPONSE

1. Possible response: It is easier to understand someone's feelings once you've experienced similar feelings.
2. Possible response: The Chinese developed porcelain hundreds of years ago. Later, the English added ash made from animal bones. This led to the name English bone china.
3. Responses will vary.
4. Possible response: Buy the kaleidoscope sooner.

EXTEND UNDERSTANDING Tell students that a *character* is someone who takes part in the events of a story. *Character traits* are the qualities of a character and are often related to personality. Select a character from the book and invite students to identify his or her traits. They must tell what elements of the story suggest that the character possesses these traits.

RESPONSE OPTIONS

WRITING Remind students that Tina's father brought along photos of his wife's teacups and memorized details about her preferences while shopping for her gift. Invite students to write about a time when they faced a similar challenge (gift-related or not) and what strategies they used to tackle it.

WORD WORK Play a game that will challenge students to identify the correct meanings of vocabulary words. Write the proper definition of each word on a separate index card while providing students with cards where they can write made-up definitions for the vocabulary (the sillier the better). Then read aloud each word along with the correct and made-up definitions for it and have students vote on the proper meaning.

SCIENCE CONNECTION

Tell students that scientists often collect objects and/or living things in order to study them. Ask why it might be helpful for scientists to have such collections on hand.

TIME FOR **Science**

Skill Work

TEACH/REVIEW VOCABULARY

Have volunteers show how the vocabulary words are used in the book. Then ask them how each word helped them better understand the story and its characters.

TARGET SKILL AND STRATEGY

MAIN IDEA The *main idea* in fiction tells what the story is about and identifies its most important ideas. Invite students to tell what this story is about and provide reasons to support their answers.

MONITOR AND FIX UP Students who *monitor* their comprehension are constantly aware of their understanding of the text. They know when the text is making sense or if their understanding of it has broken down.

Self-questioning is a strategy that can restore understanding. It involves asking oneself key questions while reading, such as, "Who is the story about? Where and when does it take place?" This strategy helps students become independent and capable readers.

Tell students that monitoring comprehension demands taking an active role in deciphering the meaning of text and thus helps them figure out the main idea of a story. Invite them to create an outline of the story to determine and keep track of its main ideas.

ADDITIONAL SKILL INSTRUCTION

REALISM AND FANTASY Explain that a *realistic story* tells about something that could happen, and a *fantasy* is a story about something that could not happen. Tell students that while they are reading they should identify specific events within *Collecting Dreams* that indicate the type of story it is. Invite them to discuss how the author could change the book to make it the other type of story.

Name _____

Main Idea

- The **main idea** is the most important idea about a paragraph, passage, or story.
- **Supporting details** are small pieces of information that tell more about the main idea.

Directions Read the following passage. Then answer the questions below.

> Tina's mother collects teacups made of English bone china. China is another name for porcelain. Porcelain was first made in China, hundreds of years ago. That is why people often call it china. For a long time the Chinese guarded the secret of how porcelain is made. But after a while their secret began to spread to other countries. Then, about two hundred years ago, the English added ash, made from animal bones, to make a special kind of porcelain called bone china.

1. In one or two words, what is this paragraph about?

_____

2. What is the main idea of the paragraph?

_____

3–4. What are the two details that tell more about the main idea?

_____

_____

_____

5–7. Imagine you are writing a paragraph about one of the characters in *Collecting Dreams*. Write the main idea of your paragraph and two details to support that main idea.

Main idea _____

Detail _____

Detail _____

Name _____

Vocabulary

Directions Choose the word from the box that best completes each sentence.
Write the word on the line.

```
┌─────────────────────────────────────────────────────┐
│            Check the Words You Know                   │
│  ___collectibles   ___credit        ___fond           │
│  ___kaleidoscope   ___porcelain     ___propped        │
│  ___rim            ___specialize    ___suspiciously   │
└─────────────────────────────────────────────────────┘
```

1. The spoon was resting on the _____ of the teacup.

2. Tina worked hard to find the perfect present, so she deserves

   the _____ for finding such a nice gift.

3. You can see beautiful colors and patterns if you look through

   a _____.

4. An antiques market is a great place for buyers to find _____.

5. The teacher looked at the boy _____ when he tried
   to hide candy in his desk.

6. She was especially _____ of long walks on warm
   summer nights.

7. Please handle the _____ dishes carefully, because they
   break easily.

8. The broom is _____ against the closet door.

9. I brought my broken antique doll to people who_____
   in repairing toys.

The Magic of Coyote

SUMMARY This is a story about the cost of being afraid and the benefit of overcoming your fear. With the help of a Navaho storyteller and a dog that is part coyote, a boy learns to conquer his fear of dogs. This story also introduces the concept of *fable,* a story with talking animals that teaches a lesson.

LESSON VOCABULARY

artifacts	breakthrough
cunning	descendant
retreated	scampered
yelping	

INTRODUCE THE BOOK

INTRODUCE THE TITLE AND AUTHOR Discuss with students the title and the author of *The Magic of Coyote.* Based on the title, ask students what they imagine this book might be about and whether the title indicates that the book is fiction or nonfiction. Note the word *magic* in the title, and discuss what it might indicate.

BUILD BACKGROUND Within this story, a Navajo storyteller shares a traditional Navajo tale about a clever coyote who teaches humans to use fire. Discuss with students other fictional tales they've encountered in which animals are smart and can talk or behave like people.

PREVIEW/USE TEXT FEATURES As students preview the book, draw their attention to the clouds pictured above the main character's head on pages 4 and 17. Ask students what these clouds mean and why they think the artist drew them. Discuss how *thought balloons* add to the story.

READ THE BOOK

SET PURPOSE Have students set a purpose for reading *The Magic of Coyote.* Students' interest in conquering their fears of dogs (or something else) should guide this purpose. Suggest that students think about the cost of being afraid and the benefits of facing their fears.

STRATEGY SUPPORT: PREDICT As students read about Henry grappling with his fear of dogs, predicting what may happen next in the story can give students a chance to reinforce what they already know. Making predictions also deepens students' involvement in the story and gives them a stake in the story's outcome.

COMPREHENSION QUESTIONS

PAGE 3 What details show you why Henry is afraid of dogs? *(They yelp and have sharp teeth and unpleasant smells.)*

PAGE 10 What clues show that Mr. Gordon's story is fiction? *(Coyote understands human conversation; coyote feels sympathy; fire beings don't really exist.)*

PAGE 21 Ranger is part coyote and part dog. Why does this help soothe Henry's fears? *(He already likes coyotes from the story. He is only afraid of the "dog" part of Ranger.)*

PAGES 21–22 What do you think the author's purpose was in having Henry pet Ranger? *(The author wanted to show that when Henry faced his fear and touched the dog, he started to get over his fear.)*

REVISIT THE BOOK

READER RESPONSE

1. Possible response: to give information about Navajo culture and to show how a story can help you get over your fears

2. Possible response: Henry will probably be much less scared around dogs. The more he is around dogs, the less frightened he will be.

3. brunch=breakfast, lunch; motel=motor, hotel; moped=motor, pedal; paratroops=parachute, troops; skylab=sky, laboratory; smog=smoke, fog: telethon=telephone, marathon

4. Responses will vary.

EXTEND UNDERSTANDING Tell students that stories that involve talking animals are common worldwide, from Aesop's fables to Navajo coyote tales to C.S. Lewis's *Chronicles of Narnia.* Encourage students to discuss what it is about animals that makes them useful as characters in stories that teach a lesson, explain an idea, or show us something about ourselves.

RESPONSE OPTIONS

WORD WORK Play a true or false word game with students. Using the vocabulary words, put the words in sentences and ask students if the words have been used correctly. For example: After the student read twenty books, she *retreated* into her room to watch TV. Do the same with all of the vocabulary words. Encourage students to write their own "true or false" sentences using the vocabulary words in this lesson.

SOCIAL STUDIES CONNECTION

Time For SOCIAL STUDIES

Invite students to learn more about the lives of Navajo children. Encourage them to use research books or the Internet. Ask them to write them short reports on what they find and to present them to the class.

Skill Work

TEACH/REVIEW VOCABULARY

Write the vocabulary words on the board. Have volunteers look up their definitions and share them with the class. Invite discussion as to how each word contributes to a story. For example, if a character is described as *cunning,* what might you expect from the character?

ELL Word studies can often make vocabulary more memorable. Demonstrate how *breakthrough* divides into *break* and *through.* Discuss the meanings of the separate words and then what they mean together. Show that *descendant* is related to *descend,* which means "to come down." Use a diagram with *grandparents* on top, then *parents,* then *children,* to show how *descend* means going down. Review that *-ed* at the end of several words makes them past tense.

TARGET SKILL AND STRATEGY

AUTHOR'S PURPOSE Remind students that the *author's purpose* is the reason why the author wrote the story. An author might want to entertain, inform, express, or persuade. Have them look for clues and details that reveal why the author might have written the story.

PREDICT Remind students that to *predict* means to guess what will happen next in a story based on what has happened before. As students read, suggest that they predict what will make Henry less afraid of dogs. Ask students to write their predictions. After they've read the story, have them review their predictions to see which ones were right.

ADDITIONAL SKILL INSTRUCTION

SEQUENCE Remind students that the *sequence of events* is the order in which events happen in a story. Have students do a story map of the book, placing major events under the headings "beginning of the story," "middle of the story," and "end of the story." As students read, ask them to write down any clue words or phrases that might help them with sequence, such as *after* or *the next day.*

Author's Purpose

- The **author's purpose** is the reason or reasons the author has for writing.
- An author may have one or more reasons for writing. Common reasons are to *inform, persuade, entertain,* or *express.*

Directions Answer the questions.

1. What do you think is the author's purpose for writing this story?

_____

_____

_____

2. What do you think is the author's purpose for including the story about Coyote?

_____

_____

_____

3. How does the story about Coyote stealing fire help Henry?

_____

_____

_____

4. What do you think the author wants you to learn about Navajo culture?

_____

_____

_____

5. Why do you think the author had Henry meet a coydog?

_____

_____

_____

Vocabulary

Directions Complete each sentence in the story with one of the vocabulary words.

Check the Words You Know

___artifacts ___breakthrough ___cunning ___descendant

___retreated ___scampered ___yelping

Henry was afraid of the (**1**) _____ dogs. Every time he saw

them, he (**2**) _____ to the back of the room.

One day, Henry and his class visited a Native American museum. First they

studied ancient (**3**) _____, such as pieces of pottery. Then it was time

for a story.

The story was told by Mr. Gordon, who was a (**4**) _____ of a

Navajo storyteller. Mr. Gordon told tales about the coyote, a (**5**) _____

creature who often played tricks on the Navajo people. Henry discovered that his

interest in coyotes made him feel less afraid about dogs. When Mr. Gordon's coydog,

Ranger, (**6**) _____ over to Henry, Henry actually petted Ranger. Henry

was excited, because he knew this was a real (**7**) _____.

Directions Write the definition of each word based on its context above.
Use a dictionary if necessary.

8. retreated _____

_____

9. breakthrough _____

_____

10. yelping _____

_____

Houses Past and Present

SUMMARY While people's basic need for shelter has not changed, America's houses certainly have changed over the past three hundred years. The author chronicles the evolution of building materials and styles from colonial thatched-roof wooden homes to today's modern fireproof structures. These different types of homes demonstrate how materials and construction techniques reflect builders' ingenuity, physical environment, and historical context.

LESSON VOCABULARY

daub	kilns	mortise
pug mill	puncheon	tallow
tenon	thatch	wattle

INTRODUCE THE BOOK

INTRODUCE THE TITLE AND AUTHOR Discuss with students the title and the author of *Houses Past and Present*. Ask them to describe homes they have seen that were built in the past and ones that have been built in modern times. Is the house shown on the cover from the past or present? How can they tell?

BUILD BACKGROUND Tell students that buildings and other shelters protect people from the weather. Invite them to think about how different kinds of shelters are particularly suited for this purpose. For example, the sloping sides and waterproof fabric of a tent repel water and keep people inside dry.

PREVIEW/USE TEXT FEATURES Ask students to leaf through the pages and look at the photos. Based on these images, what can they tell about how the size, shape, materials, and construction of houses have changed over the years?

READ THE BOOK

SET PURPOSE Have students set a purpose for reading *Houses Past and Present*. Their knowledge of houses from long ago and modern times should guide this purpose. Suggest that they think about how houses reflect the environments and technology of different time periods.

STRATEGY SUPPORT: ASK QUESTIONS *KWL* stands for "What I *Know*," "What I *Want* to know," and "What I *Learned*." Before reading, create a KWL chart on the board about houses from long ago and current times. Ask readers to share what they already know about such homes and come up with questions about what they would like to know about them. Have students look for answers to their questions as they read and then tell what they have learned about houses. Record all responses in the appropriate columns.

COMPREHENSION QUESTIONS

PAGE 8 Why did colonists use moss, leaves, and mud for building log cabins? *(They stuffed these materials between logs in their cabins to keep out cold air.)*

PAGE 10 Is the following sentence a statement of fact or opinion? *Early colonial fireplaces were much bigger than they are today.* Explain why. *(Fact. Colonial fireplaces can be measured and compared to modern ones.)*

PAGE 11 By the 1700s how did colonists build strong homes without using nails or pegs? *(They used a mortise-and-tenon method to connect the wood.)*

PAGE 16 Why did prairie settlers build homes of sod instead of lumber? *(There were no forests for lumber.)*

REVISIT THE BOOK

READER RESPONSE

1. Possible response: The stone chimney, shake shingle roofs, and tile roofs did not catch fire, thus preventing homes from burning.
2. Possible responses: "How was your home built? Where did you learn your building skills?"
3. Responses will vary.
4. It shows what a mortise and a tenon look like, and you can see how they fit together.

EXTEND UNDERSTANDING Ask students to carefully study the close-up photos and diagrams of construction materials and building techniques. Discuss how they help students understand house-building in colonial times.

RESPONSE OPTIONS

WRITING Ask students to pretend they are builders from the 1700s. Have them write a "how-to" manual on building or maintaining a colonial home.

WORD WORK Tell students that homographs are words that are spelled the same but have different meanings and different origins. Have students look up *wattle,* and point out that there are separate listings for the two different meanings. Tell students that this is how you can recognize a homograph. Have them look up *bark, mail, compound.*

ELL Have students draw a picture of a house from the past or present and then write bilingual labels or captions for its parts.

SOCIAL STUDIES CONNECTION

Time For SOCIAL STUDIES

Invite students to consult books and other reference materials on different types of shelters around the world. Ask them to make drawings and write about what makes each shelter well-suited for its setting.

Skill Work

TEACH/REVIEW VOCABULARY

Have students create bookmarks where they can list new words they discover while reading. On the bookmarks they may write their names, the book title, the new words, and the page numbers on which they appeared. After reading, review some of the words as a class.

TARGET SKILL AND STRATEGY

DRAW CONCLUSIONS Ask students to use what they read plus common sense and experience to *draw conclusions* about houses past and present. Suggest that they use diagrams such as a simple web or a blank chart to write facts and personal knowledge that support a conclusion.

ASK QUESTIONS Remind students that good readers *ask questions* about what they read to predict, to understand, and to think about what they have learned. Model: Before reading: *I wonder what this will be about?* or *I really want to know about. . . .* During: *I wonder what this means. I'll read it again to find out* or *I like this. How did the author make it so exciting?* After: *What did I like best?* or *I wonder where I can learn more about. . . ."* Remind students that asking questions will help them draw conclusions as they read the book.

ADDITIONAL SKILL INSTRUCTION

FACT AND OPINION A statement of *fact* can be proven true or false by consulting reference books and using other evidence. An *opinion* is a judgment or belief that cannot be proven true or false but should involve the use of thoughtful judgment. Tell students that nonfiction books such as *Houses Past and Present* are mostly about statements of fact. Invite students to identify examples in the book and reference sources that can be used to verify these statements of fact. Then ask students to make statements of opinion about what they have read.

Draw Conclusions

- When you **draw conclusions** you use what you have read and what you already know to make reasonable decisions about characters or events.

Directions Read the following passage. Then answer the questions below.

During the pioneer era of the 1800s, settlers moved west to the prairie lands. There were no forests of tall trees to cut down for lumber. So these settlers found a way to use the ground itself to make their first homes. All around them was the grass of the prairie. The grass had deep roots which held the dirt below it.

Settlers used plows to cut through the grass-covered ground, or sod. With a plow they were able to dig the grass up in long strips. Then they cut the strips of sod into sections. The pieces of sod were stacked like bricks to build the walls of the shelter.

1. Which of the following statements is a reasonable conclusion about settlers living in prairie lands?

   a. Settlers loved their sod houses.

   b. Building sod houses is easy.

   c. Settlers had to adapt to their new environment in order to survive.

2. Which of the following statements is NOT a reasonable conclusion about settlers living in prairie lands?

   a. Settlers had to work very hard to build their sod homes.

   b. Sod houses could be dirty and filled with insects.

   c. Sod houses offered a comfortable, luxurious home.

3. How do you think settlers felt about living in sod houses? Why do you think so?

   _____

   _____

4. How might settlers have built their homes differently if there were trees? Why?

   _____

Name _____

Vocabulary

Directions Write the word from the box that matches each definition below.

Check the Words You Know		
___daub	___kilns	___mortise
___pug mill	___puncheon	___tallow
___tenon	___thatch	___wattle

1. _____ grasses, leaves, or straw used to cover a roof

2. _____ animal fat used to make candles

3. _____ a type of flooring made up of halved logs

4. _____ very hot ovens used for making bricks

5. _____ a hole in one piece of wood that helps form a joint with another wooden piece

6. _____ sticks interwoven with twigs and branches

7. _____ the end of a piece of wood that fits into the hole described in item 5.

8. _____ a coating of plaster, clay, mud, or any other sticky material

9. _____ a hollow tub with knives used for mixing and grinding clay

Directions Write a sentence about houses past and present. Use as many vocabulary words as you can.

_____

_____

_____

Nicky's Meadow

SUMMARY A boy misses his suburban garden when his family moves to the city. Readers experience urban environments that have a variety of plants. Cause and effect relationships emerge as Nicky is shown New York City's greenery.

LESSON VOCABULARY

abandoned	artificial
astonished	concerned
glum	sprouting
statue	waddling

INTRODUCE THE BOOK

INTRODUCE THE TITLE AND AUTHOR Discuss with students the title and the author of *Nicky's Meadow*. Point out the "Science" triangle on the cover and discuss how the book might fit into that category. Ask students to describe Nicky's expression and how it might give clues about the story.

BUILD BACKGROUND Ask students to share their experience with plants and trees. Explain that most plants start from seeds and need sunlight and water to grow. Guide the discussion to include different places that have many plants and trees, such as parks, forests, farms, and meadows.

PREVIEW/USE ILLUSTRATIONS Invite students to look at the story's illustrations, and ask them what they imagine the story will be about. Tell them to notice the change in Nicky's expression as the story continues and discuss what his expressions suggest.

READ THE BOOK

SET PURPOSE Have students set a purpose for reading *Nicky's Meadow*. Students' interests in gardening and any experience they have with moving should guide this purpose.

STRATEGY SUPPORT: STORY STRUCTURE Review with students that story structure is how a story is organized. Point out that the events in this story are in a chronological sequence. Then prompt students to complete a time line as they read *Nicky's Meadow*.

COMPREHENSION QUESTIONS

PAGES 3–5 What caused Nicky to be sad about moving? *(He didn't want to leave his house, his garden, or the neighborhood.)*

PAGE 7 Why do you think the author chose this illustration for the cover? *(Possible response: Nicky looks sad, and the illustration makes you want to read to find out why.)*

PAGE 17 What is a green roof? *(a roof made out of grass and planted in dirt)*

REVISIT THE BOOK

READER RESPONSE

1. He hopes it will remind Nicky of the meadow.
2. Central Park, the rooftop garden, the community, the farmers market, the railroad track
3. When Nicky uses the word *artificial*, he means *fake*. He is saying that Central Park is not like a natural meadow.
4. Responses will vary.

EXTEND UNDERSTANDING Remind students that *characters* are the people who do the action in a story and that often characters change. Ask: What kind of person was Nicky at the beginning of the story? How and why did he change by the end?

RESPONSE OPTIONS

WRITING Ask students to imagine they are Nicky two years after he moved to New York City with his family. Have students write a letter to friends in Ohio explaining how they feel about living in the city now.

SCIENCE CONNECTION

Invite students to research other kinds of gardens, such as bonsai or waterless plants. Ask them to write a report about the garden and to illustrate it.

Skill Work

TEACH/REVIEW VOCABULARY

Review vocabulary words with students. Then scramble the letters of each word and have students unscramble them. Prompt students to use the vocabulary words in a sentence.

ELL Review vocabulary words with students. Then ask them to write each word on one side of an index card and its definition on the other side. Pair students and have them quiz each other using the cards.

TARGET SKILL AND STRATEGY

CAUSE AND EFFECT Remind students that *cause* is why something happened and *effect* is what happened. Remind students that a cause can have more than one effect, such as "Because it rained, the game was canceled, and we stayed home." Pause while reading and prompt students to identify cause and effect relationships by asking, "What happened? Why did it happen?"

STORY STRUCTURE Remind students that *story structure* is the way a story is organized, and that in this story the structure is chronological—events are described in the order that they happened. Remind students that understanding the story's structure can help them recognize causes and effects. Then select four events from the story and write each on an index card. Give students the cards and ask them to put the events in order.

ADDITIONAL SKILL INSTRUCTION

MAIN IDEA Remind students that the *main idea* is the most important idea of a story, passage, or paragraph. Sometimes the author states the main idea, and other times readers must identify it and say it in their own words. Prompt students to find the main idea as they read *Nicky's Meadow*.

Cause and Effect

- A **cause** is *why* something happened.
- An **effect** is *what* happened.

Directions The box below lists Effects found in *Nicky's Meadow*. For each Cause below, write the letter of its Effect.

Effects	
a. Nicky's whole family had to move there.	e. He grew food there.
b. Another boy would have to help her.	f. He went to say goodbye to his meadow in Ohio.
c. Nicky's uncle took him to Central Park.	g. Nicky began to think that New York was fun.
d. He decided to show Nicky a meadow in New York City.	h. Nicky tried to eat with chopsticks.

Cause	Effect
1. Nicky was sad about leaving Ohio.	
2. Nicky could not help Mrs. Margolis if he lived in New York.	
3. Nicky's father got a job in New York City.	
4. Nicky worried there wouldn't be grass in New York.	
5. Nicky's family went to a Chinese restaurant.	
6. Max had land in a community garden.	
7. Nicky and his grandfather went to the farmer's market.	
8. Nicky's grandfather knew Nicky missed his meadow.	

© Pearson Education 3

Vocabulary

Directions Write the definition of each vocabulary word.

Check the Words You Know

___abandoned   ___artificial   ___astonished   ___convinced
___glum   ___sprouting   ___statue   ___waddling

1. abandoned _____

2. artificial _____

3. astonished _____

4. convinced _____

5. glum _____

6. statue _____

7. sprouting _____

8. waddling _____

Directions Answer the questions using complete sentences.

9. Why was Nicky glum?

_____

_____

10. What things in New York City astonished Nicky?

_____

_____

11. What convinced Nicky that New York might not be such a bad place to live?

_____

_____

55

Star Tracks

SUMMARY This nonfiction book provides information about constellations and celestial navigation and shows how scientists explain and study nature. The book gives a history of how sailors navigated by the stars, leading to the invention of the telescope. Students are also introduced to important astronomers such as Galileo, Sir Isaac Newton, and George Hale, the inventor of the Hubble telescope.

LESSON VOCABULARY

astronomers	celestial navigation
constellations	dead reckoning
galaxy	latitude
light-year	quadrant
refractive	telescope

INTRODUCE THE BOOK

INTRODUCE THE TITLE AND AUTHOR Introduce students to the title and the author of *Star Tracks*. Based on the title, ask students what kind of information they think this book will provide. Ask: Are you familiar with the instrument the girl on the cover photograph is using? How does the title of the book give you clues to what she is doing?

BUILD BACKGROUND Ask students if they have ever looked through a telescope or seen any of the photographs from the Hubble telescope. Then discuss with students if they and their family have ever gotten lost and what signposts they might have looked for to help them find their way. Tell students that by reading this book, they can find out about how people navigate using the stars.

PREVIEW/USE ILLUSTRATIONS Suggest students skim the text and look at the illustrations and captions. Ask: What clues do these text elements give as to what this book might be about?

READ THE BOOK

SET PURPOSE Have students set a purpose for reading *Star Tracks*. Students' interest and curiosity about stars and celestial navigation can guide this purpose. As students read, suggest they take down notes that might provide answers to any questions they might have about the subject.

STRATEGY SUPPORT: SUMMARIZE To give students more support in summarizing, ask them to summarize the previous school year or their summer vacation. Remind students that as they read, they can take notes that summarize what they are reading and give clues to the author's purpose in writing the story.

COMPREHENSION QUESTIONS

PAGE 7 Why is the North Star so important for celestial navigation? *(It is always found by looking north.)*

PAGES 10–11 Summarize how early explorers used the stars to navigate. *(Early explorers depended on the sun and on the stars. Then they used dead reckoning to measure their course.)*

PAGE 13 Summarize why it's difficult to depend on the quadrant to navigate. *(The North Star is sometimes hidden by clouds; the horizon can be difficult to find in the dark; ocean waves make it difficult to hold a quadrant steady.)*

PAGE 16 What do you think the author's purpose is in telling you that Galileo was not at first believed? *(to express the notion that because people do not believe something does not mean that it is not true)*

TALK ABOUT THE BOOK

READER RESPONSE

1. Possible response: The author's purpose was to explain how important stars are in the universe and what people have done to find out more about them.
2. Galileo built a powerful telescope. He proved Copernicus's theory that the sun is the center of the universe. He used his telescope to learn more about the planets and the stars.
3. Possible responses: *television, telephone, telethon*. Sentences will vary.
4. The picture shows that you need to place your eye up against the sextant in order to make it work.

EXTEND UNDERSTANDING Remind students that *cause* is why something happened and *effect* is what happened. Ask students to write down the causes of celestial navigation in one column and the effects in another column.

RESPONSE OPTIONS

WRITING Ask students to imagine that they are Galileo and are making a short commercial trying to persuade people that the moon is bumpy. Have students write a short script and act it out for the class.

SCIENCE CONNECTION

Hand out drawing paper on which dots for Orion and Leo are drawn. Invite students to create their own constellation pictures for these groups of stars. Then suggest they do more research on the constellations and write a few lines about them on the bottom of their drawings.

TIME FOR
Science

Skill Work

TEACH/REVIEW VOCABULARY

Review the vocabulary words. Then, to reinforce their definitions, make a "vocabulary star map." Create two five-pointed stars with a vocabulary word at each point. Have students write the meanings of the words along the lines of the stars. When students are finished, have them cut out their stars and hang them in a "vocabulary constellation" on a bulletin board.

ELL Give students a list of definitions and have them match the definition with the correct vocabulary word.

TARGET SKILL AND STRATEGY

AUTHOR'S PURPOSE Remind students that an *author's purpose* is the reason an author writes a story, such as to inform, to entertain, to express, or to persuade. Invite students to discuss why they think an author might write about the stars. Ask: What do you think the author might like you to know?

SUMMARIZE Remind students that *summarizing* is retelling the main idea of a story in a few sentences. To practice the skill, give students short paragraphs to summarize.

ADDITIONAL SKILL INSTRUCTION

FACT AND OPINION Remind students that a statement of *fact* can be proven true, and a statement of *opinion* is someone's view and can be true or not true. To give students practice, give them several sentences, some fact and some opinion, and have them mark each as such. Then have students write their own statements of fact and opinion about a topic they choose.

Name _____

Author's Purpose

- The **author's purpose** is the reason or reasons an author has for writing.
- An author may have one or more reasons for writing. He or she may want *to inform, to entertain, to persuade,* or *to express* a mood or feeling.

Directions Reread *Star Tracks*. Then answer the questions about author's purpose below.

1. Why do you think the author began this reader by describing driving to a soccer match when you don't know the way?

_____

_____

2. Why did the author include a passage about Columbus?

_____

_____

3. What does the author want you to know about early explorers and the sky?

_____

_____

4. On page 10, why did the author want you to think about how the ocean looked at night?

_____

_____

5. What did the author want you to know about Galileo?

_____

_____

Name _____

Vocabulary

Directions The vocabulary words are hidden in the box of letters. Find and circle the words.

Check the Words You Know

___astronomers   ___celestial navigation
___constellations   ___dead reckoning
___galaxy   ___latitude
___light-year   ___quadrant
___refractive   ___telescope

```
C O N S T E L L A T I O N S Q I N A
E L O I C R Y R S M S L U P F M N X
L A R C D L L A T I T U D E T K L P
E J I T E U I M R P S P C R V C B U
S L O E Y A G D O O T Y F I Z Y I D
T P P L E L H E N E O T E R P O O E
I L T E T A T T O P O R O M G F S A
A Y L S T Y Y L M V D M K I S G Z D
L E M C M E E E E S H A G E U A Z R
N I U O S T A O R E F R A C T I V E
A V W P A V R R S O M Y L L B D S C
V V W E A V I Q U A D R A N T M R K
I I U L S T R O O Z P I X T F A T O
G V W J A V I R Z O M Y Y L S P W N
A V W J A V I R O X M Y P L A D T I
T J I T E U I M R P S P C R V C B N
I L O U Y A G D O O T Y F I Z Y I G
O P P R E L H E N E O T E R P O O N
N L T E T A T T O P O R O M G F S G
```

Follow Me! How People Track Animals

SUMMARY This nonfiction book explores what people can learn about animals by tracking how, when, and where they move. Also included are details about different methods scientists use to better understand animals.

LESSON VOCABULARY

analyze	biologists
classify	data
hibernating	mammal
measurement	migrate
scat	tranquilizers

INTRODUCE THE BOOK

INTRODUCE THE TITLE AND AUTHOR Discuss with students the title and the author of *Follow Me! How People Track Animals*. Based on the title, ask students what kind of information they think this book will provide. Ask: Why do you think the book is called *Follow Me! How People Track Animals*? Who does the *me* refer to, the trackers or the animals? Direct students to look at the cover illustration and ask them what clues this gives about the selection.

BUILD BACKGROUND Ask students if they have ever seen birds flying south for the winter or returning in the spring and if they know why birds migrate. Discuss with students what they know about other migrating animals and how they know it, such as from documentaries or other sources.

PREVIEW/USE TEXT FEATURES Invite students to skim the book and look through the photographs, illustrations, map, and captions. Ask how these elements give students an idea of the book's organization and content.

READ THE BOOK

SET PURPOSE Have students set a purpose for reading *Follow Me! How People Track Animals*. Students' curiosity about migrating animals or about wildlife in general should guide this purpose. Suggest that as they read, students take notes about the different migrating animals.

STRATEGY SUPPORT: ASK QUESTIONS As they read, have students answer the questions they posed earlier. When they finish reading, ask students if they have more questions. Suggest they write their new questions and research the answers.

COMPREHENSION QUESTIONS

PAGE 4 How can you tell if a Grizzly has been nearby? *(Grizzlies leave their scent on trees, strip bark, and leave their fur behind.)*

PAGES 8–9 What two conclusions can you draw about why biologists might not use radio collars anymore? *(There are many modern methods that scientists use today; it's difficult and dangerous to put collars on bears unless they are hibernating.)*

PAGE 21 What questions do you have about tracking insects? *(Possible response: How does the Doppler radar track them? Do all insects migrate? Where do they migrate?)*

PAGE 21 Why is it important to track migrating animals? *(Possible response: We can learn a lot about nature by tracking these animals.)*

REVIST THE BOOK

READER RESPONSE

1. Possible response: The bird was captured by biologists, who then tagged and released it.
2. Possible responses: Are there ways to track bats other than by using mist nets? What happens to the glow sticks that get used? What do mist nets look like? Can bats see them?
3. Possible response: The page talks about microchip transmitters being placed under a snake's skin, so they must be very small. Also the book is about tracking, so it must be some kind of device that helps people track animals.
4. The diagram shows how the signal is transmitted.

EXTEND UNDERSTANDING Remind students that *sequence* is the order in which events occur in a story. Ask students to write down the sequence of tracking one of the animals featured in the selection. Remind them that writing down the sequence can help them remember and summarize what they have read.

RESPONSE OPTIONS

WRITING Ask students to imagine they are an animal being tracked by biologists. Ask them to write a one- to two-page letter to the animal's relatives describing their experiences of being tracked.

SCIENCE CONNECTION

Have students choose a migrating animal and write a short report on where, how, and when the animal migrates. Encourage students to visit the library and use the Internet. Have students present their reports to the class.

Skill Work

TEACH/REVIEW VOCABULARY

After reviewing vocabulary with students, use the words to play several rounds of hangman. Once students guess a word, ask them to supply the definition and use the word in a sentence.

ELL Ask students to skim the text and write down any words they don't understand. Help them find the meanings of these words in the dictionary and prompt them to use the words in sentences.

TARGET SKILL AND STRATEGY

DRAW CONCLUSIONS Remind students that *drawing conclusions* means reaching a decision that makes sense after thinking about facts and details. Give students a short article from a magazine or newspaper and ask them to draw conclusions about it. Suggest that students write the facts and details that support their conclusions.

ASK QUESTIONS Remind students that *asking questions* is a way to further understand a topic. Have students write questions they have about what they expect to read. Suggest that as they read, students jot down details that supply the answers to any of their questions.

ADDITIONAL SKILL INSTRUCTION

COMPARE AND CONTRAST Remind students that *comparing* means finding the similarities of things and *contrasting* means finding the differences. Suggest that students compare and contrast cats and dogs, focusing on how animals are alike and how they differ. Graph the findings on the board.

Name _____

Draw Conclusions

- **Drawing conclusions** is thinking about facts or details and deciding something about them.
- It can also mean figuring something out by thinking about it.

Directions Draw a conclusion about each sentence. Then write a conclusion sentence.

1. John ran away from Tim's dog.

_____

2. Judy put on her warm coat and gloves.

_____

3. Zelda reread the story before writing her report.

_____

Directions Write a paragraph about tracking animals. Then draw a conclusion based on the information you provided.

_____

_____

_____

_____

_____

_____

_____

_____

Conclusion: _____

_____

Vocabulary

Directions Circle the letter of the sentence in which the vocabulary word has been used correctly. Then write the definition of the vocabulary word.

Check the Words You Know

___analyze	___biologists	___classify	___data	___hibernating
___mammal	___measurement	___migrate	___scat	___tranquilizers

---

1. **a.** The biologists spent three months looking for the information.

   b. Her arteries were clogged with biologists.

   _____

2. **a.** Be careful not to disturb the hibernating bear.

   b. The hibernating bears frolicked in the waterfall and caught fish.

   _____

   _____

3. **a.** We collected data about trees for our special report.

   b. Please put the data in the refrigerator where they belong.

   _____

4. **a.** A dinosaur is not a mammal, but a human being is.

   b. I read twenty pages of the mammal.

   _____

   _____

5. **a.** Please don't analyze the food into such small pieces.

   b. We need to analyze the information and determine what it means.

   _____

   _____

Whales and Other Animal Wonders

SUMMARY This book introduces students to the way in which scientists study animals, especially whales. It also introduces readers to scientists' findings about wolves and other canids, gorillas, chimps, and endangered apes.

LESSON VOCABULARY

canids	cetacean
echolocation	flukes
marine biologists	primate
sonar	species

INTRODUCE THE BOOK

INTRODUCE THE TITLE AND AUTHOR Discuss with students the title and the author of *Whales and Other Animal Wonders*. Ask students why a book on animals might have the word *wonders* in its title. Allow them to discuss why or why not animals can be called *wonders*.

BUILD BACKGROUND Discuss students' interest in how scientists approach animals. For instance, marine biologists study why whales beach and how their system of echolocation works. Some scientists go to habitats and observe animals.

PREVIEW/USE TEXT FEATURES Encourage students to look at the captions, sidebars, and charts to get a sense of what animals will be covered in this book. As students look at the photos of the different animals, ask which of the animals they have seen.

ELL Ask students who have had the opportunity to be around animals to volunteer to make up a radio script about these animals. The script should introduce young people to a scientist's way of observing animals.

READ THE BOOK

SET PURPOSE Draw on students' natural interest in animals when asking them to set a purpose for reading the book. They may look at the cover and decide they want to know more about one animal than another. Remind them that nonfiction books often contain much information, so setting a purpose will help keep them focused as they read.

STRATEGY SUPPORT: ANSWER QUESTIONS By asking your students questions before they read, you are helping them to learn more from their reading. It also allows them to be more accurate in their understanding of the text. This accuracy aids a student's ability to formulate several facts or ideas into one generalization.

COMPREHENSION QUESTIONS

PAGE 5 Why do many scientists believe that human noise has much to do with why whales beach? *(Human noise and the use of submarine sonar have increased over the years, and the number of beached whales has also increased.)*

PAGES 7, 19 What can be said about animals communicating? *(Whales communicate by echolocation and clicking sounds; some gorillas and chimps communicate with sounds and gestures.)*

PAGE 11 Why are there more coyotes today? *(As the number of wolves decreases, there are fewer to attack coyotes as prey, allowing coyotes to increase.)*

PAGES 12–13 Why are scientists' attempts to put wolves back into the United States working well? *(Scientists are keeping track of where the wolves are; the wolves are reproducing in the wild.)*

REVIST THE BOOK

READER RESPONSE

1. Responses will vary.
2. Sometimes human activities interrupt whales echolocation.
3. The two words are *echo* and *location.* Together, *echolocation* means using a sound to locate something.
4. three baleen whales: blue, right, and humpback whales

EXTEND UNDERSTANDING As students research endangered species on the Internet and at the library, suggest that they research animals that scientists have prevented from becoming extinct. Read about how scientists and other people, like us, helped this effort.

RESPONSE OPTIONS

WRITING/SPEAKING Suggest that students think about what animal interests them the most. Have them research information from a section of the book and write two paragraphs about that animal. Some students might prefer to give an oral report in pairs on the topic they have researched.

SCIENCE CONNECTION

TIME FOR Science

Invite students to make their own chart of animals and the aspects of them that scientists study. Encourage students to find different ways that scientists study animals, such as observing how whales react to human sounds and teaching animals to communicate. Have students look for ways that are different from those suggested in the book.

Skill Work

TEACH/REVIEW VOCABULARY

As the students read this book, notice which words they find most difficult or intriguing. Students interested in echolocation may want to research the subject and tell the class more about scientists' findings. Some students may be interested in the work of marine biologists and can report on what it takes to be one. Others may research words having to do with canids or other dog-like animals.

TARGET SKILL AND STRATEGY

GENERALIZE Because this reader presents a number of facts and examples about animals, students will need to organize the information in order to *generalize* the topic. To express what the animals have in common, students' generalizations should show likenesses by using clue words such as *many, most, generally, overall,* etc.

ANSWER QUESTIONS Remind students how important it is to let questions prompt them and to *answer questions* as they read. This strategy helps them think actively about their reading. Questions help them generalize and express the main ideas from the text that they read.

ADDITIONAL SKILL INSTRUCTION

AUTHOR'S PURPOSE Explain that *author's purpose* is the reason or reasons an author has for writing. Because every author's goal is to communicate, authors often have more than one purpose for writing. Review with students the four typical reasons—to persuade, to inform, to entertain, and to express mood or feeling. Open a discussion by asking what two reasons the author of this book might have had in mind. *(to inform, to entertain)* Ask students to support their answers.

Generalize

- When authors present one statement about many ideas or people, they **generalize**. A generalization is a kind of conclusion.
- Clue words such as *all*, *many*, *none*, and *usually* show a generalization.

Directions For each generalization below, list two facts that support it. Use *Whales and Other Animal Wonders* to help you.

- There are many ways a whale can end up beached.

1. _____

2. _____

- Many human activities can cause whales to beach.

3. _____

4. _____

- Imbalances in nature generally create problems.

5. _____

6. _____

- Wolves and dogs have many similarities that make them good pets.

7. _____

8. _____

- Many animals other than dogs make interesting pets.

9. _____

10. _____

Vocabulary

Directions Draw a line from each vocabulary word to its definition.

Check the Words You Know

___canids   ___cetacean   ___echolocation   ___flukes

___marine biologists   ___primate   ___sonar   ___species

1. primate

2. species

3. cetacean

4. flukes

5. marine biologists

6. canids

7. sonar

8. echolocation

a. dog-like animals

b. a marine animal that breathes through a blowhole

c. sending out waves to find objects

d. halves of whale's tail

e. a method for detecting sound underwater

f. mammals that are among the most intelligent beings on Earth

g. scientists who study ocean plants and animals

h. a system for classifying animals

Directions Write a paragraph about whales using as many vocabulary words as possible.

_____

_____

_____

_____

_____

_____

_____

Earth Movement

SUMMARY This book gives readers information about current technology that predicts earthquakes and volcanic eruptions. It also shows how science protects us from natural disasters.

LESSON VOCABULARY

fault

instrument

monitor

observatory

volcanologist

fumes

magma

network

prehistoric

INTRODUCE THE BOOK

INTRODUCE THE TITLE AND AUTHOR Discuss with students the title and the author of *Earth Movement*. Draw their attention to the type treatment of the word *movement*. Ask: Why do you think the illustrator curved the letters that way? What does the shape make you think of? What feelings do you get when you look at the photograph on the cover?

BUILD BACKGROUND Ask students if they have ever predicted the weather. Discuss how they made their predictions and whether they came to pass. Then ask students what they know about natural disasters like earthquakes and volcanic eruptions. Discuss any movies or photographs of such events they have seen.

PREVIEW/USE TEXT FEATURES Direct students' attention to the diagrams and maps throughout the reader. Point out how these features are a different way to explain material. Direct students' attention to page 8, and ask them how this particular diagram makes it easier to understand how a volcanic eruption happens.

READ THE BOOK

SET PURPOSE Have students set a purpose for reading *Earth Movement*. Students' interest in earthquakes and volcanoes should guide this purpose.

STRATEGY SUPPORT: MONITOR AND FIX UP Remind students that as they read the selection, they should use their monitor and fix-up graphic organizer and fill it in as they read. Tell students they can also use fix-up strategies such as reading ahead or reading slowly.

COMPREHENSION QUESTIONS

PAGE 8 How does this diagram help you understand how a volcano happens on all sides? *(It shows the earthquake under the volcano, the gasses above, and the bulge on the side.)*

PAGE 9 Did you understand what *magma* meant here? If not, go back and reread this page and look at the glossary. (Magma *is melted rock within the earth.)*

PAGE 14 Why is it easier to predict an earthquake than a volcano? *(It is easier to predict a volcano. Earthquakes don't give off warning signs.)*

PAGES 14–15 Compare and contrast predicting volcanoes and earthquakes. *(Compare: Scientists know a lot about where they are likely to happen. Contrast: Volcanoes give off warning signs, and earthquakes do not.)*

REVISIT THE BOOK

READER RESPONSE

1. Diagrams should show that students comprehend differences between volcanic eruptions and earthquakes.
2. By measuring changes in the slant of the ground, tiltmeters help scientists predict volcanoes.
3. Possible responses: It was my *fault* that the dish broke.
4. Students might say that the images helped them understand where the fault is located and the direction in which it slides.

EXTEND UNDERSTANDING Ask students how subheads help them understand the purpose of the book's diagrams and maps. Show how diagrams make difficult information easier to understand. Direct students' attention to the maps on pages 14 and 16, and discuss how the maps organize information about earthquakes.

ELL Ask students questions that get them personally involved by using them as the subject of questions relevant to the article. *(What would you study if you were a volconologist?)*

RESPONSE OPTIONS

WRITING Ask students to imagine they are scientists getting ready to monitor a volcano. Suggest they write out a "To Do" list and give reasons why each item is listed.

SCIENCE CONNECTION

Suggest students do more research on famous volcanic eruptions such as Vesuvius or Krakatoa. Have students write reports, illustrate them, and present them to the class.

Skill Work

TEACH/REVIEW VOCABULARY

To reinforce the contextual meanings of words like *observatory*, suggest students read the passage on page 7 that includes the word. Ask what details show them this instrument is special. Do this with all vocabulary words.

TARGET SKILL AND STRATEGY

COMPARE AND CONTRAST Remind students that comparing and contrasting means showing how things are alike and how they are different. Remind students that many words can offer clues to comparisons and contrasts, such as *however, different, unlike, similarly,* and *but.* Give students a topic such as "rainy days and snowy days," and ask them to compare and contrast using clue words.

MONITOR AND FIX UP Remind students that *monitoring* their comprehension as they read means being aware of their comprehension and recognizing when the text stops making sense to them. When students run into comprehension problems, *fix-up* strategies such as rereading can help.

Give students a graphic organizer with the headings *If This Happens* and *Then I Can Expect That To Happen,* and encourage them to use it when they are confused. Explain how the strategy of compare and contrast can help them with their understanding.

ADDITIONAL SKILL INSTRUCTION

DRAW CONCLUSIONS Remind students that a conclusion is a decision or opinion reached after thinking about some facts and details. Give students a graphic organizer with the headings *What You Know, Text Clues,* and *Conclusions.* Suggest that as they read, they fill out the chart and then *draw conclusions* about earthquakes.

Name _____

Compare and Contrast

- To **compare** two or more things means to find the similarities and the differences.
- To **contrast** two or more things means to find the differences.
- Clue words, such as *like*, *however*, *differently*, *similarly*, and *but* help you identify similarities and differences.

Directions Reread *Earth Movement*. Use the Venn Diagram below to compare and contrast earthquakes and volcanoes.

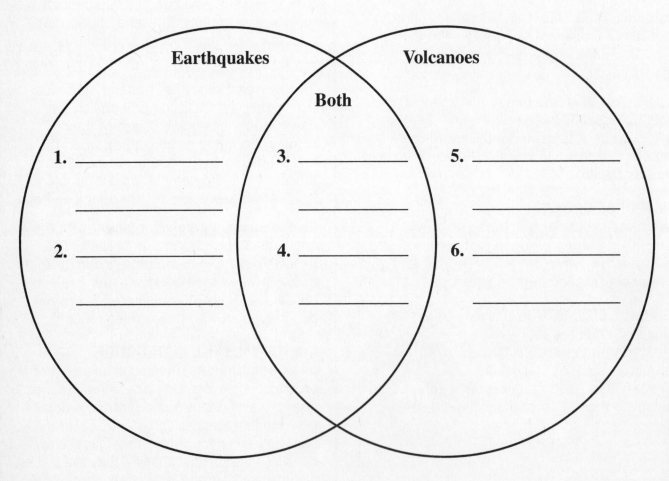

Earthquakes   **Volcanoes**

Both

1. _____

2. _____

3. _____

4. _____

5. _____

6. _____

Vocabulary

Directions Complete the crossword puzzle. First look at the clues below. Then write the correct vocabulary word in the puzzle.

Check the Words You Know

___fault   ___fumes   ___instrument
___magma   ___monitor   ___network
___observatory ___prehistoric ___volcanologist

DOWN

1. A person who studies volcanoes
2. To track the changes
3. From the time before written history
4. A place used for making observations

ACROSS

5. Smoke-like gasses
6. A group of connected things
7. A break in the crust of the earth
8. Hot molten earth
9. A special tool

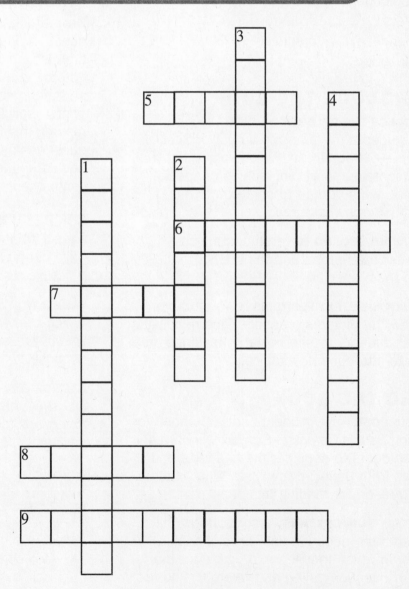

SUMMARY This nonfiction book profiles specially gifted people of renown. By presenting some life difficulties associated with their talents, the book extends the lesson concept of how being unique makes someone lonely.

LESSON VOCABULARY

appreciated	courageous
dedication	extraordinary
feats	opportunities
pioneer	prejudice
struggled	triumph

INTRODUCE THE BOOK

INTRODUCE THE TITLE AND AUTHOR Discuss with students the title and author of *Special Talents—Extraordinary Lives*. Explain that the book contains short biographies of special people. Ask students to name other biographies they may have read.

BUILD BACKGROUND Have students discuss their favorite heroes and the talents that make them special.

PREVIEW/USE TEXT FEATURES Have students preview the pictures, captions, and headings. Guide students to see how the headings are used to introduce new topics.

READ THE BOOK

SET PURPOSE Have students set a purpose for reading *Special Talents—Extraordinary Lives*. Ask students to consider the headings and photos from their preview. Ask: What is a good reason for reading this book?

STRATEGY SUPPORT: ANSWER QUESTIONS Teach students the question-answer relationship (QAR), in which they learn to figure out the type of question asked and where to find the information to answer it. Teach the four types of questions:

· Right There: The answer is in one sentence in the text.
· Think and Search: The answer is in several different sentences throughout the text.
· Author and You: The reader needs the text plus prior knowledge to find the answer.
· On My Own: The answer is not in the text. The reader uses his or her prior knowledge instead.

Have students read page 3, then write this question on the chalkboard: How many people are discussed in this book? Have students determine the type of question (Right There) and then find the answer (eight). Have students apply QAR before, during, and after reading this book by having them answer your questions as well as the questions in the book's Reader Response and in this guide's comprehension questions.

COMPREHENSION QUESTIONS

PAGE 6 What kind of trouble might Jefferson have been in if Britain had won the war? *(Possible response: He might have been jailed.)*

PAGE 9 Why was Dsickinson's life so different? Which clue word helps you know? (*Her style of writing was so extraordinary. The clue word is* because.)

PAGE 13 Why didn't Jackie Robinson give up? *(Possible response: He wanted African Americans to be able to play in the major leagues.)*

PAGE 20 Do you think using their talents was worth the difficulties these talented people faced? Why or why not? *(Possible response: Yes. It is more important to be your best.)*

REVISIT THE BOOK

READER RESPONSE

1. Cause: Galileo designed a powerful telescope. Effect: Galileo was arrested and punished.
2. Possible response: Life is great, because they can do what they love. Life is hard, because they are not understood and they must make sacrifices. I based my answer on the lives of the people in this selection.
3. Possible response: He *struggled* to read the long book. Her *extraordinary* skating made her famous.
4. Possible response: Emily Dickinson, because she believed in herself when others doubted her.

EXTEND UNDERSTANDING Have students look at the quoted poem on page 9. Explain that biographers often include examples of a subject's writings to help the reader understand the subject's work. The examples are sometimes set apart from the text to help the reader focus.

RESPONSE OPTIONS

WRITING Have students write a paragraph that summarizes one of the eight stories in the book.

SOCIAL STUDIES CONNECTION

Time For SOCIAL STUDIES

Have student pairs research the life of one of the people profiled in this book. Have them create an immediate family tree for that person to display in class.

Skill Work

TEACH/REVIEW VOCABULARY

Form student pairs. Have each partner write a cloze sentence for one of the vocabulary words. Ask partners to exchange sentences and fill in the correct word. Have students repeat the activity until all the words have been used at least once.

ELL Make one set of cards for the vocabulary words and another set for their definitions. Have students play a memory game by pairing words and definitions.

TARGET SKILL AND STRATEGY

CAUSE AND EFFECT Remind students: An *effect* is something that happens. A cause is why that thing happens. Model: "After page 5, I ask, 'What happened?' Galileo was arrested. 'Why did it happen?' Talking about his discovery was against the law." Have students use a cause-and-effect graphic organizer to keep track as they ask "What happened?" and "Why did it happen?" as they read this book.

ANSWER QUESTIONS To *answer questions* teach students the question-answer relationship (QAR), in which they learn to figure out the type of question asked—Right There, Think and Search, Author and You, or On My Own—and where to find the information to answer it. Have students apply QAR by having them answer questions related to the text. Remind students that they can apply QAR to questions about cause-and-effect relationships.

ADDITIONAL SKILL INSTRUCTION

DRAW CONCLUSIONS Remind students that a *conclusion* is a decision you reach that makes sense after you think about details or facts in what you read. Model: On page 8, I read that Emily Dickinson did not change her style to get published. I think that Dickinson believed that being true to her style was more important than being famous. Encourage students to draw conclusions as they read.

Name _____

Cause and Effect

- A **cause** is why something happened. An **effect** is what happened. Look for clue words such as **because, so, it, then,** and **since.**

Directions Reread this passage from *Special Talents—Extraordinary Lives.*

> Sometimes a genius like Galileo is a pioneer, or the first person ever to do something. Before Galileo, no one had looked at the Sun through a telescope, so no one knew that it was harmful to the eyes. That may have been why Galileo lost his eyesight. But being a pioneer also got Galileo into trouble with the law.
>
> In the 1600s in Italy, people believed that the Sun revolved around Earth. Even though Galileo was right, hardly anyone believed him. Because talking about his discovery was against the law, Galileo was arrested. As punishment, he had to stay inside his house for the rest of his life.

Use the information from the passage to fill in the graphic organizer.

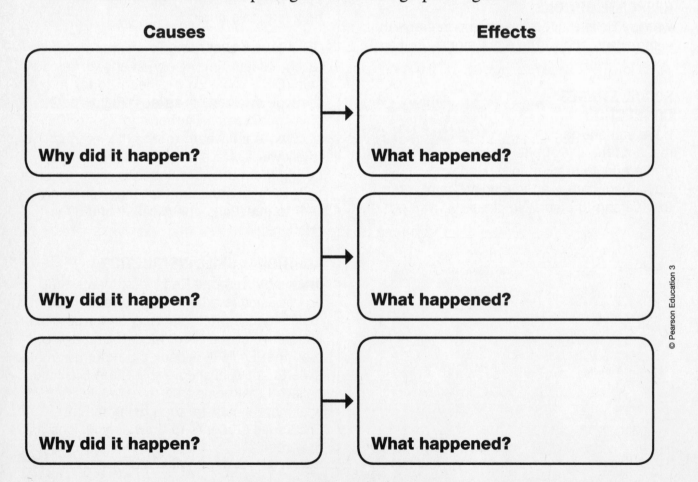

Causes

Effects

Why did it happen?

What happened?

Why did it happen?

What happened?

Why did it happen?

What happened?

Name _____

Vocabulary

Directions Write the word that matches the definition.

1. _____ *n.* a person who does something no one else has done before

2. _____ *n.* great and constant interest in something

3. _____ *n.* victory or success after great effort

4. _____ *adj.* full of courage; fearless

5. _____ *n.* good chances to do things; convenient occasions

6. _____ *v.* thought highly of; recognized the worth of; valued

7. _____ *v.* tried hard; worked hard against difficulties

8. _____ *n.* acts that show great skill, strength, or daring

9. _____ *n.* an opinion or judgment formed unfairly or without knowing all the facts

10. _____ *adj.* very unusual; remarkable; special

Fastest, Longest, Biggest, Lightest

SUMMARY *Fastest, Longest, Biggest, Lightest* tells the story of *Guinness World Records,* the famous compendium of trivia. This nonfiction reader describes how the book originated, how records are verified and entered into the book, and what sorts of records the book contains.

LESSON VOCABULARY

accomplishment	compendium
existing	positive
procedure	superlative
translated	trivia
verified	

INTRODUCE THE BOOK

INTRODUCE THE TITLE AND AUTHOR Discuss with students the title and the author of *Fastest, Longest, Biggest, Lightest.* First, talk about what the words in the main title all have in common. Then, have students read the subtitle, *The Guinness World Records Story,* and invite students to tell what they know about *Guinness World Records.*

BUILD BACKGROUND Discuss with students the meaning of the word *record.* Ask students to name any famous records they know. *(Possible responses: Tallest mountain is Everest; Barry Bonds holds the record for most homeruns in a baseball season.)* Talk with students about how these records are measured. Have students suggest records that might be hard to check, such as the oldest person, and explain why they think checking the record would be difficult. Then discuss where a person might look for records such as these.

PREVIEW/USE TEXT FEATURES If students are unfamiliar with *Guinness World Records,* explain that this reader is about a book that contains thousands of records in many categories. Have students skim through the reader and look at the pictures and captions. Ask: What sorts of records does this reader talk about?

READ THE BOOK

SET PURPOSE To help students set purposes for reading, invite them to think of one question that they would like to ask about *Guinness World Records.* Have students read to find answers to their questions.

STRATEGY SUPPORT: ASK QUESTIONS Invite students to suggest questions that could help them find and describe comparisons and contrasts in the text *(Possible responses: What records seem the same? Which records seem different?)* Write the questions on the board. Tell students to use these questions to find and explain their comparisons and contrasts.

COMPREHENSION QUESTIONS

PAGE 4 Besides informing the reader, what do you think is the author's purpose for describing the largest spider and the fastest fish? *(Possible response: entertaining the reader with interesting trivia from the book)*

PAGE 6 The sizes of birds' eggs are compared on this page. What else does the author compare or contrast? *(She contrasts Earth's coldest temperature with its average temperature.)*

PAGES 8–9 What questions do you still have after reading these pages? Where could you look for answers? *(Possible responses: What are some of the languages that* Guinness World Records *is translated into? I could look in the library or the book itself.)*

PAGES 16–18 What steps would you need to take to get into Guinness World Records? *(think of a record to set or break, write to* Guinness World Records *and describe your idea, wait for them to write and accept your idea)*

REVISIT THE BOOK

READER RESPONSE

1. *Same:* both involve bird eggs; *Different:* one was from an ostrich and the heaviest egg ever and the other was from a canary and the lightest egg ever.
2. Possible response: Which bird could fly faster, the golden plover or the grouse? The question wasn't answered.
3. Super; Possible response: *Super* means the best. *Superlative* means something with the best qualities.
4. 2.2 pounds

EXTEND UNDERSTANDING Have students look through the pictures in the reader once again. Point out that even though this is a nonfiction book, the illustrations look like cartoons. Discuss with students why drawings like these may have been used and how the illustrations add to their understanding or enjoyment of the book.

RESPONSE OPTIONS

WRITING Have students think of records that they would like to set for *Guinness World Records.* Provide students with copies of the book and tell them to check whether their ideas are already in the record book. Then have students write out their ideas on copies of the *Guinness World Record* idea forms. Have students share their ideas.

SCIENCE CONNECTION

Have students make a class list of some natural records they expect to find in *Guinness World Records,* such as driest place, greatest snowfall, most hurricanes. Have students make predictions about what parts of the world will hold these records and put them on a chart. Then have students check the records in the book. Tell them to plot the locations of these "bests" on a map of the world and list them in their natural records chart. Discuss as a class which predictions were correct and which incorrect and which records were most surprising.

Skill Work

TEACH/REVIEW VOCABULARY

Read through the Glossary with students. Pair students and have each partner write three clues for each word. Clues can be definitions, parts of speech, pronunciations, synonyms, antonyms, or spelling. Then have partners exchange clues and try to guess the words without using the Glossary.

TARGET SKILL AND STRATEGY

COMPARE AND CONTRAST Remind students that when they *compare* and *contrast* things, they are talking about how they are alike and different. Review with students that authors may compare and contrast two or more things with or without clue words such as *like, as, but, however.* Have students read to find one example of a comparison or contrast that the author makes and one that they make themselves.

ELL Have ELL students complete a *Comparison and Contrast Chart* with the following column headings: *Record: How Record Was Measured; Nature, Animal, or Human Record.* Help students complete the chart for two records in the reader.

ASK QUESTIONS Point out to students that they can ask questions to compare and contrast things in a story. Suggest to students that they ask themselves questions as they read that will help them find comparisons and contrasts.

ADDITIONAL SKILL INSTRUCTION

AUTHOR'S PURPOSE Review with students that an *author's purpose* is the author's reason for writing a text. Remind students that while many nonfiction authors write with the purpose of informing the reader about something, they may also write with another purpose: to entertain, persuade, or express. As they read, have students figure out what other purpose Kirsten Anderson may have had, besides informing the reader, for writing *Fastest, Longest, Biggest, Lightest.*

Compare and Contrast

- A **comparison** shows how two or more things are alike. A **contrast** shows how two or more things are different.
- Clue words such as **like** and **as** show comparisons. Clue words such as **but** and **unlike** show contrasts.

Directions Read the following passage. Then answer the questions below.

What about the huge spider that we first asked about? According to the book, the biggest spider ever was found in 1965. It measured eleven inches across. That's the size of a large frying pan! | And what about the world's fastest fish? The book says that the cosmopolitan sailfish has been measured at speeds of 68 miles per hour. A fish that fast can keep up with a car on a highway!

1. What does the author compare the spider to?

_____

2. How does the comparison help you to understand what you read about the spider?

_____

_____

3. What does the author compare the fastest fish to?

_____

4. How does the comparison help you to understand what you read about the fish?

_____

_____

5. Summarize how both comparisons helped you to understand what you read.

_____

_____

_____

Vocabulary

Directions Choose a word from the word box that has the same meaning as the underlined words. Write the word on the line.

1. I like to read books that contain <u>fun and amusing facts</u>. _____

2. The <u>book that gave a lot of information in a small space</u> took a long time to read.
   _____

3. The runner's world record could not be <u>proved true</u>. _____

4. You should be very proud of your <u>special thing that you did</u>.
   _____

5. A <u>way of doing something</u> should be followed carefully in a science experiment.
   _____

Directions For each word or phrase below, choose a word from the word box that has the opposite meaning. Write the word on the line.

6. proved false _____

7. average _____

8. failure _____

9. in the same language _____

10. extinct _____

A Gem of a Tale!

SUMMARY *A Gem of a Tale!* describes the 12 gemstones that serve as traditional birthstones. This nonfiction reader includes pictures of each gem, descriptions of its qualities, and details about where the gem is found in the world.

LESSON VOCABULARY

birthstone	brilliant	crystal
flaws	minerals	mined
quartz	rockhounds	transparent

INTRODUCE THE BOOK

INTRODUCE THE TITLE AND AUTHOR Discuss with students the title and the author of *A Gem of a Tale!* Ask students if they recognize the stone in the cover photograph. (diamond) Point out the content triangle, and talk about why a book featuring diamonds would relate to science.

BUILD BACKGROUND Put the word *gem* at the center of a content web. Invite students to suggest all the words that come to mind when they think of the word *gem*. Suggest that they think not only about the finished product, but where gems come from. Then tell students that the selection they are about to read will describe some well-known gems.

PREVIEW/USE TEXT FEATURES Have students look through the pictures, charts, and map in the book. Ask what students expect to learn from the book about gems. *(information about the twelve birthstones that belong to each month, where the birthstones are found, how they are formed)*

ELL Invite ELL students to talk about gems that are found in their home countries or are important to their families' cultures. Have volunteers describe the gems and why they are considered special or valuable to their families and friends.

READ THE BOOK

SET PURPOSE Use the Prior Knowledge activity to guide students to set a purpose for reading. Remind students to think about what they would like to know about gems and birthstones. Then have them choose what they would most like to learn, and invite them to read to find out more about this topic.

STRATEGY SUPPORT: PRIOR KNOWLEDGE To help students activate prior knowledge, have each student create a KWLS chart with the headings, What I Know, What I Would Like to Know, What I Learned, and What I Still Want to Know. Students can use the ideas from the concept web about gems to fill in the Know column together. Then ask students to fill in the second column with the facts they would like to learn about gems and birthstones. Tell students to complete the last two columns of the chart when they have finished reading the selection.

COMPREHENSION QUESTIONS

PAGE 4 What is the effect of cutting and polishing gemstones? (makes them sparkle and shine)

PAGES 6–7 Make a generalization about where gemstones are found. *(Possible response: Many gemstones are found in the southern part of Africa.)*

PAGE 11 What prior knowledge helped you understand the information on this page? *(Possible response: I know what a diamond looks like, so I could imagine how hard it is.)*

PAGE 14 Why do you think there is a picture of the British Crown Jewels on this page? *(Possible response: The page is about rubies, so there are probably rubies in the Crown Jewels.)*

PAGE 19 What generalization does the author make on this page? *(Most of the blue topaz that we see today has been treated with light.)*

REVISIT THE BOOK

READER RESPONSE

1. Yes, even though there are some places in the world where gemstones are not found, it is true that they are found in many places.
2. Possible responses: I knew that a diamond is the hardest stone. I wanted to know more about my birthstone, amethyst. I learned that my birthstone is in the British Crown Jewels.
3. Possible responses: My grandmother wore her stunning birthstone ring to the opera. The rockhound searched for shiny, green emeralds in North Carolina.
4. Africa and Asia

EXTEND UNDERSTANDING

Have students analyze the structure of the sections in pages 8–19 to identify how each section is set up. Elicit that each section consists of a photograph of the gemstone, its name and related month, textual discussion of the gemstone that identifies where it is found, and another photograph that highlights an interesting fact about the gemstone.

RESPONSE OPTIONS

VIEWING Show students images of some of the precious gems at the Smithsonian Museum of Natural History, including the Hope Diamond and the British Crown jewels. Have students write brief paragraphs describing which gems are their favorites and why.

SCIENCE CONNECTION
Explain to students that geologists are people who study the physical nature of the earth and rocks. Tell students to imagine that they are geologists. Have each student choose a gem described in the text, such as their birthstone, and find out how their gem is formed.

Skill Work

TEACH/REVIEW VOCABULARY
Read through the Glossary with students. Have each student find a picture of his or her birthstone in the reader. Ask students to use the pictures and the vocabulary words to write paragraphs describing their stones.

TARGET SKILL AND STRATEGY

GENERALIZE Remind students that sometimes authors make a general statement about several ideas or things in a book. This statement, called a generalization, can tell how the ideas or things are all alike or mostly alike, or how the ideas or things are mostly different. Point out that certain clue words, such as *all, many, most, always, some, usually, seldom, few,* or *in general,* may alert students to generalizations that an author makes. Have students look for generalizations that the author makes as they read.

PRIOR KNOWLEDGE Remind students that their prior knowledge is what they already know about a topic. Point out that prior knowledge can help them understand generalizations that an author makes in a text or even help them make their own generalizations. Review with students the concept web about gems on the board. Have students use this prior knowledge to make some generalizations about gems before they read.

ADDITIONAL SKILL INSTRUCTION

CAUSE AND EFFECT Review with students that an effect is what happens and a cause is why that event happens. To figure out the cause of something, a reader may have to ask questions such as "Why did this probably happen?" Have students think about the qualities of the gems described in the book, and tell them to suggest what caused these gemstones to be assigned as birthstones.

Generalize

- A **generalization** is a broad statement about several ideas or things in a book.
- A **valid generalization** is adequately supported by specific facts and by logic.

Directions Read the passage below.

Most gems are formed from minerals. To become a gem, a mineral must cool and harden into a solid crystal. Crystals are minerals that have special shapes and patterns.

When they are first discovered and mined, most gems look like ordinary rocks. They are often rough and unevenly shaped. In the hands of talented gem cutters, however, these raw chunks of mineral become brilliant gemstones. The best gemstones are often made into jewelry.

Gemstones are like snowflakes. No two are exactly the same. Gemstones come in every color of the rainbow. When they are cut and polished, gemstones' colors sparkle and shine. The gemstones that sparkle and shine the most are worth the most money!

Directions Write three generalizations the author makes about gemstones in this passage. For each generalization, write a detail from the passage that supports the generalization.

1. Generalization: _____

   2. Supporting Detail: _____

3. Generalization: _____

   4. Supporting Detail: _____

5. Generalization: _____

   6. Supporting Detail: _____

Name _____

Vocabulary

Directions Use eight words from the box to complete the puzzle below.

Check the Words You Know

___birthstone	___brilliant	___crystal	___flaws	___mined
___minerals	___quartz	___rockhounds	___transparent	

Across:

2. very bright and shiny

4. defects or blemishes

5. the nickname given to people who hunt, dig, and collect rocks and gems

6. a gemstone associated with one of the twelve months of the year

7. a very hard mineral found in many different types of rock

Down:

1. a hard, solid piece of some substance that is naturally formed of flat surfaces and angles

3. allowing light to pass through

8. dug up from under the ground

A Time of Change

SUMMARY This reader provides the biographies of many women who broke down barriers during the late nineteenth and early twentieth centuries. The selection details the efforts of these pioneers to open doors for women in politics, education, sports, the workforce, and other aspects of life.

LESSON VOCABULARY

accepted	convention	criticized
limited	opportunities	pioneers
prejudiced	suffrage	

INTRODUCE THE BOOK

INTRODUCE THE TITLE AND AUTHOR Discuss the title and the author of *A Time of Change: Women in the Early Twentieth Century*. Make sure students understand the dates of the time period mentioned in the subtitle and covered in the book: 1900 to about 1945.

BUILD BACKGROUND Discuss with students what they know or think life was like for women in the early twentieth century. Talk about society's expectations in the early 1900s—that a woman's primary role was to take care of a household and raise a family. Then have students compare what life was like 100 years ago to what it is like for women today. Invite volunteers to describe some of the activities in which women and girls participate outside of the home.

PREVIEW/USE TEXT FEATURES Have students skim through the book, focusing on the *headings*, *sidebars*, *pictures*, and *captions*. Ask students if they recognize any of the women in the pictures. Discuss with students what they think the book will be about, based on these pictures and the topics mentioned in the headings, captions, and sidebars.

ELL Invite volunteers to describe some of the women pioneers from their own cultures. Provide some examples from students' home countries if students cannot think of examples themselves.

READ THE BOOK

SET PURPOSE Review with students the women and topics they expect the book to cover, based on their preview. Have students choose the women or topics about which they would like to learn more.

STRATEGY SUPPORT: MONITOR AND FIX UP To reinforce monitor and fix-up strategies, have students stop reading briefly at the end of every section. Tell them to monitor their understanding by asking themselves questions such as, "What did the author just tell me about? Who or what was important in that section?" Have students keep a list of the points in the story that confuse them and the fix-up strategies they use to clarify information. List some fix-up strategies on the chalkboard as reminders to students during reading.

COMPREHENSION QUESTIONS

PAGE 3 Find one statement of fact and one statement of opinion on this page. How do you know the difference? (Possible responses: Fact: Also, once a woman married, any property she owned became her husband's. I can research to prove it true or false. Opinion: But it was also an exciting time. It's the author's belief and I can't prove it.)

PAGES 6–7 Did you find anything confusing on these pages? What did you do to fix up your understanding? (Possible response: I didn't know what the word declaration meant, but I read on and used context clues to guess that it meant a document that states ideas.)

PAGES 12–13 What is one generalization the author makes? (Possible response: Most doctors were still men.)

PAGE 16 What statement of opinion does the author make about some women in the early 1900s? (Possible response: Women pioneers did amazing things.)

PAGES 18–19 Name one statement of fact in these pages. Where could you check to prove the statement true or false? *(Possible response: In 1934, Lettie Pate Whitehead became the director of the Coca-Cola Company. I could check the Coca-Cola Web site.)*

REVISIT THE BOOK

READER RESPONSE

1. Possible responses: Facts: In 1900, women could not vote. Elizabeth Cady Stanton started the Women's Rights Movement. Opinions: Women should stay home with children. Women were not as smart as men.
2. Possible responses: I reread the section. I turned the subhead into a question and read to find the answer. Examples will vary.
3. Responses will vary.
4. Elizabeth Cady Stanton, because she helped plan the first Women's Rights Convention in 1848 and wrote its "Declaration of Sentiments"

EXTEND UNDERSTANDING Point out that authors of nonfiction often use headings to help readers understand information or recognize the main idea of a section. Review with students the headings in *A Time of Change*. Discuss how the headings help the reader understand the information in each section and recognize the author's main ideas.

RESPONSE OPTIONS

WRITING AND SPEAKING Have each student choose one of the women featured in the book and imagine that she is receiving a "Woman of the Century" award. Direct each student to write a speech introducing the person and explaining why she is a good choice for the award. Have students give their speeches to the class.

SOCIAL STUDIES CONNECTION

Time For
SOCIAL
STUDIES

Have students research and write biographies of other pioneers of the twentieth century. Tell students that their subjects may be women, African Americans, young people, leaders in a field, or anyone else who was the first to accomplish something important. Compile the biographies into a *Who's Who of the Twentieth Century*.

Skill Work

TEACH/REVIEW VOCABULARY

Read through the Glossary with students. Direct students to think about whether each word makes them think of happy, positive ideas or unhappy, negative ideas. As a class, have students group the words based on whether they have positive or negative connotations. Tell students to explain their decisions.

TARGET SKILL AND STRATEGY

FACT AND OPINION Explain to students that a *statement of fact* can be proved true or false and can be checked by looking in reference sources, by asking an expert, or even by observing. A *statement of opinion* is a person's beliefs or ideas about something. Point out to students that opinions often contain clue words such as *I believe, in my opinion, best, worst, most, should,* and other judgment words. Give examples of statements of fact and statements of opinion, and discuss with students how to distinguish between the two. Direct students to look for facts and opinions in the text.

MONITOR AND FIX UP Review with students that they should *monitor* their reading, or check their understanding of the text. Remind students that when they don't understand something, they can use a strategy to *fix up* their reading. Provide examples of common fix-up strategies, such as rereading, reading on, scanning, using text features, and taking notes. Explain that using monitor and fix-up strategies may help them understand facts and opinions in the text. Have students monitor their reading and note the fix-up strategies they use to help their comprehension.

ADDITIONAL SKILL INSTRUCTION

GENERALIZE Review with students that when they *generalize*, they are making a broad statement that applies to a group of things or ideas. Provide students with some generalizations and clue words, such as *every, all, most, few, never*. As they read, have students find generalizations that the author makes.

Fact and Opinion

- A statement of **fact** is a statement that can be proved true or false. You can check a statement of fact by looking in reference sources, asking an expert, or observing.
- A statement of **opinion** is a person's beliefs or ideas about something. You cannot prove whether it is true or false.

Directions Use the book *A Time of Change* to answer the questions below.

1. Reread page 4 in the book. What is a statement of fact on this page?

_____

_____

2. What is one statement of opinion that the author makes on page 4? How do you know that this is an opinion and not a fact?

_____

_____

_____

3. Reread the section of the book entitled "Women in College." What is one statement of fact that the author makes about colleges for women in the 1800s?

_____

4. What is a statement of opinion that the author makes about women in college during the early 1900s?

_____

_____

5. Reread the Conclusion, beginning on page 20 in the reader. Which statement contains both a fact and an opinion? Which part is which?

_____

_____

_____

_____

Vocabulary

Directions For each word below, separate the word into its base word and its ending. Then write a sentence using the base word. Use a dictionary to help you.

1. prejudiced

Base word _____

Ending _____

Sentence with base word _____

_____

2. criticized

Base word _____

Ending _____

Sentence with base word _____

_____

3. accepted

Base word _____

Ending _____

Sentence with base word _____

_____

4. opportunities

Base word _____

Ending _____

Sentence with base word _____

_____

5. limited

Base word _____

Ending _____

Sentence with base word _____

_____

Directions Imagine you are a woman attending the first Women's Rights Convention in 1848. On a separate sheet of paper, write a diary entry about your experience there using the words *convention, pioneers, prejudiced,* and *suffrage.*

Smart Dog

SUMMARY This story, about a boy wanting to teach his dog Toby to sit, shows students that dogs can learn to do some things but that other things are done by natural instinct.

LESSON VOCABULARY

brightened   commanded
familiar   promise
scampered   suspicious
trotted   twitched

INTRODUCE THE BOOK

INTRODUCE THE TITLE AND AUTHOR Discuss the title and author of *Smart Dog* with students. Ask students, based on the cover illustration and the title, what they think this story is about.

BUILD BACKGROUND Ask students if they have ever had a dog or a pet or if they have known someone who had a dog or a pet. Discuss what students know about how and what animals learn.

PREVIEW Invite students to look through the story illustrations. Ask students how the illustrations give them an idea of what the story is about. Direct students' attention to the illustration on pages 22–23. Ask students if they think this drawing indicates that there will be a happy ending to the story.

READ THE BOOK

SET PURPOSE Have students set a purpose for reading *Smart Dog*. Students' curiosity about dogs and their natural instincts should guide their purpose.

STRATEGY SUPPORT: GRAPHIC ORGANIZERS Suggest that as students read *Smart Dog*, they create two or three graphic organizers to enhance their understanding of the story. For example, they could use a story map for the plot; a time line for the sequence of events; character webs to describe Charlie, Toby, Eileen, and Mom; or a problem-and-solution or cause-and-effect chart to understand the action in the story.

COMPREHENSION QUESTIONS

PAGE 5 What story detail makes you think that Charlie may not be able to teach Toby a trick? *(Toby dug up the flowers.)*

PAGES 6–7 Which plot events are important on these pages, and which plot events are not? *(Possible responses: Important: Training Toby was Charlie's biggest goal. Charlie tried to teach Toby to sit. Toby failed but didn't give up. Unimportant: It had taken Mom and Dad a long time to let Charlie have a dog. Charlie met lots of dogs at the shelter.)*

PAGE 13 What details show you the kind of person Charlie was? *(Possible responses: He was responsible, because he cleaned up his dog's digging. He was sensitive, because he felt sad that Mom yelled.)*

PAGE 23 What do you think the author wants you to know and understand about natural instinct and learning? *(Possible responses: I think the author wants me to know that dogs can learn some things, but they do other things by instinct. Sometimes instinct can help a dog to learn.)*

REVISIT THE BOOK

READER RESPONSE

1. Events: Charlie got Toby. Charlie tried to teach Toby a trick. Toby learned his name. Big Idea: It takes time to train a dog.
2. Instinct: digging in dirt, grabbing for biscuit, chasing squirrel, following scent to get home. Learned behavior: lying still, sitting, responding to name
3. Words should be used as adverbs, and sentences should demonstrate understanding of vocabulary.
4. Possible responses: sit, walk alongside owner (heel), stop walking, roll over, not jump on people, not beg for food

EXTEND UNDERSTANDING Remind students that a character is a person or animal who takes part in the events of a story. Suggest that students make a character web about Charlie. Putting Charlie's name in the center circle, have students write events in the story that show what Charlie does, what Charlie says, and what others say about Charlie. Based on the finished character web, ask students to discuss what they know about Charlie and to predict what Charlie might do next.

RESPONSE OPTIONS

WRITING Invite students to pretend they are Toby the dog and have them write a letter to Charlie explaining why it seemed to take so long to learn the things Charlie wanted.

SOCIAL STUDIES CONNECTION

Time For SOCIAL STUDIES

Suggest that students research and write about how seeing eye dogs are trained and how they bond with their visually impaired owners.

Skill Work

TEACH/REVIEW VOCABULARY

Scramble the spelling of each vocabulary word and write the scrambled words on the chalkboard in one column. In another column write the definitions in a different order. Have students unscramble each word and copy its correct definition from the chalkboard.

ELL For each vocabulary word, give students a sentence where the vocabulary word is used correctly and one where it is used incorrectly. Have the student choose the correct sentence.

TARGET SKILL AND STRATEGY

PLOT AND THEME Remind students that the plot consists of the events at the beginning, middle, and end of a story. Also tell students that a story usually has a big idea, or lesson to learn. Suggest that as students read *Smart Dog*, they should use a story map to outline the story's plot and big ideas.

GRAPHIC ORGANIZERS Remind students that graphic organizers are charts or diagrams that help students understand what they read. Have students use prior knowledge to make a KWL chart. Have them fill in the first section, "What I Know," and the second section, "What I Want to Know." Suggest that as students read, they fill in the last section, "What I Learned." Remind students that using a graphic organizer can help them determine the plot and the big idea of the story.

ADDITIONAL SKILL INSTRUCTION

CHARACTER AND SETTING Remind students that a character is the person or animal that does the actions in the story, and that setting is the time and place where the story occurs. Remind students that the setting of a story can influence how a character behaves. Suggest that, as they read, students make notes about how the setting influences what Charlie does.

Plot and Theme

- The **plot** of a story is made up of the important things that happen. The plot can be divided into 3 parts—beginning, middle, and end.
- The **theme** of a story is the big idea. It is an idea that the author would like you to learn. The theme can be stated in one sentence.

Directions The theme of *Smart Dog* is that it takes time and effort to train a dog. Circle the events below that relate to the theme. Then decide if each happened in the beginning, middle, or end of the story. Write your answer on the line.

1. _____ Toby's ears perked up. He knew that *he* was Toby and that Charlie was calling *him*.

2. _____ Eileen shrugged. "That's all right. I'm glad he's home, even if he is just a silly dog."

3. _____ "If you can teach him a trick in one week, I'll set the table and wash and dry the dishes every night."

4. _____ Toby ran through the opening of the gate and into the front yard.

5. _____ Toby flopped down lazily and rolled over to have his stomach scratched.

6. _____ Charlie's friend Nina came to visit the next day. She had an idea about how to train Toby.

7. _____ Toby heard his name. He turned around and trotted straight over to Charlie.

8. _____ The next day, Charlie rode his bike to the library and looked for books about dog training.

9. _____ The week was almost over and Toby hadn't learned a trick yet.

10. _____ Charlie pulled Toby from the garden and frantically tried to push the dirt back into place so that Mom wouldn't notice.

Name _____

Vocabulary

Directions Choose a word from the word box to answer the questions below.

```
Check the Words You Know

___brightened        ___commanded
___familiar          ___promise
___scampered         ___suspicious
___trotted           ___twitched
```

1. Which word describes someone getting happier? _____

2. Which word describes something that isn't quite right? _____

3. Which word describes the perky way a dog might have walked? _____

4. What word describes something you say you will absolutely do? _____

5. Which word describes how a rabbit wiggled its nose? _____

6. Which word describes something you are used to? _____

7. Which word describes someone who gave orders? _____

8. Which word describes how a mouse ran into a hole? _____

Directions Write a sentence for each of the words below.

9. suspicious

_____

_____

10. brightened

_____

_____

The Japanese Language

SUMMARY This selection gives students information about Japanese writing, language, culture, and body language. It provides a fascinating way to compare and contrast our culture with the Japanese way of life.

LESSON VOCABULARY

diagram	discord
harmony	ideal
isolated	linguists
mainland	unique

INTRODUCE THE BOOK

INTRODUCE THE TITLE AND AUTHOR Discuss with students the title and cover of *The Japanese Language*. Ask students if they know what the girl on the cover is doing and how it differs from the way American students write—and the materials they write with.

BUILD BACKGROUND Ask students what they know about Japanese culture and language. Point out that we use some Japanese words, such as *sushi* and *kimono*. Discuss with students why different cultures have different languages.

ELL Invite English learners to teach the class a few words from their native language, and to talk about their culture to the class.

PREVIEW/USE TEXT FEATURES Suggest that students look through the photographs, charts, and maps and discuss what information these give about the text. Direct students' attention to page 4 and discuss the Japanese words and characters for various numbers.

READ THE BOOK

SET PURPOSE Have students set a purpose for reading *The Japanese Language*. Students' interest in and curiosity about different cultures and languages, or about Japan, should guide this purpose.

STRATEGY SUPPORT: PREDICT/CONFIRM PREDICTIONS As students read, remind them to use their graphic organizers to make predictions and to check back to see if their predictions were correct. Suggest that students revise their predictions based on any new information they might read.

COMPREHENSION QUESTIONS

PAGE 10 What are some of the rules of our culture that you can think of? *(Possible responses: We respect families and one another's religions, it is important to get a good education.)*

PAGE 11 Compare and contrast Japanese vowels with English vowels. *(Both share* a, e, i, o, u, *but English also has* y.*)*

PAGE 14 Read the description of Japanese gardens and draw a conclusion from it. *(Possible response: Japanese gardens are made in harmony with nature, which is a cultural value.)*

PAGE 18 To show respect, what kinds of body language and speech do Americans use when they greet one another? *(Possible response: Americans stand up, look people in the eye, and reach out to shake hands.)*

REVISIT THE BOOK

READER RESPONSE

1. Possible responses: Japanese: new words came from China; Both: many rules for making words and sentences; English: new words came from Latin.
2. Possible response: Yes, Japanese will continue to change because it has changed throughout its history. Languages are always changing.
3. Japanese people follow rules for speaking and behaving. People show respect by choosing the right words and knowing when to speak.
4. Responses will vary.

EXTEND UNDERSTANDING Direct students' attention to pages 22 and 23. Ask students to try and write Kanji and then ask them how an activity like this helps them to better understand *The Japanese Language*.

RESPONSE OPTIONS

WRITING Based on what students now know and understand about Japanese language and culture, invite them to write a short play about a young student who learns how to speak correctly to a respected teacher.

SOCIAL STUDIES CONNECTION

Time For SOCIAL STUDIES

Invite students to make up their own language. Have them write a few words of their new language and draw a picture for each word. Then students can see if other students can tell what the word is from the drawing.

Skill Work

TEACH/REVIEW VOCABULARY

Review vocabulary words with students. Scramble the letters of each word and invite students to unscramble the word, give its definition, and then use the word in a sentence.

TARGET SKILL AND STRATEGY

COMPARE AND CONTRAST Remind students that a *comparison* shows how two or more things are alike. A *contrast* shows how two or more things are different. Remind students that a simile is a comparison that uses the clue word *as* or *like,* while a metaphor is a comparison that does not use those words. Invite students to create similes and metaphors about winter and summer. Suggest that students use a graphic organizer with the headings "English" and "Japanese" to help them compare and contrast as they read *The Japanese Language*.

PREDICT/CONFIRM PREDICTIONS Remind students that *predicting* means to guess what will happen next based on what they have read already. Ask students to predict what they think *The Japanese Language* might teach them. Suggest that students use a graphic organizer as they read to jot down details that either support or change their prediction. Remind students that making predictions can help them compare and contrast.

ADDITIONAL SKILL INSTRUCTION

DRAW CONCLUSIONS Remind students that *drawing a conclusion* is reaching a decision or opinion that makes sense after thinking about some facts or details. Suggest to students that as they read they think about the details and make decisions about what might happen next in the selection. To give students practice, ask them to think about drawing a conclusion about why it's important to go to school. Suggest students make a diagram to illustrate the facts that led them to their conclusions.

Compare and Contrast

- A **comparison** shows how two or more things are alike.
- A **contrast** shows how things are different.
- **Similes** use the clue word *as* or *like* to compare two things that may seem very different.
- **Metaphors** are comparisons that do not use *as* or *like*. Here are examples of each.

Directions Read the examples of similes and metaphors in the box. Then write four similes and four metaphors.

Similes	Metaphors
She was pretty as a picture.	The world is a stage.
The day was as hot as a fire.	He is a beast.
He was busy as a bee.	School is a training ground.
She sang like a bird.	

_____

_____

_____

_____

_____

_____

_____

_____

Vocabulary

Directions Write a story about Japan based on what you read. Be sure to use all the vocabulary words in your story.

Check the Words You Know

___diagram   ___discord   ___harmony   ___ideal
___isolated   ___linguists   ___mainland   ___unique

_____

_____

_____

_____

_____

_____

_____

_____

_____

_____

_____

_____

_____

Living Abroad

SUMMARY This reader is about the many reasons Americans choose to live overseas for long or short periods. Their reasons are many: to work, to study, to live with another family, to serve in the military, or to volunteer. People who live abroad like to learn about other countries, languages, cultures, and customs.

LESSON VOCABULARY

abroad	ancient
anthropologists	archeologists
deployed	stationed
transferred	volunteers

INTRODUCE THE BOOK

INTRODUCE THE TITLE AND AUTHOR Discuss with students the title and the author of *Living Abroad*. Ask students to describe what they imagine this book will be about based on the title and the cover photograph.

BUILD BACKGROUND Ask students whether any of them have lived overseas. If so, have them talk about where they lived, why they were there, and how long they stayed. If there are any students who grew up in a foreign country, have them talk about what it was like for them to come to the United States. Have all students imagine where in the world they would like to live most.

PREVIEW/USE TEXT FEATURES Have students look at the headings and photographs, and discuss how these text elements help organize the book. Ask students how previewing the headings can help them understand what this book is about.

READ THE BOOK

SET PURPOSE Have students set a purpose for reading *Living Abroad*. For example, they may want to focus on the reasons people choose to live abroad. Their curiosity about foreign countries can guide them in setting their purpose.

STRATEGY SUPPORT: TEXT STRUCTURE To give students more support in learning to recognize text structure, have them write one sentence that summarizes the main idea of each section, and jot down a few notes about details that support the main idea of each section.

COMPREHENSION QUESTIONS

PAGE 9 How does the text define what a diplomat is? (*government workers who represent the United States abroad*)

PAGE 11 How can being an exchange student help you learn another language? (*opportunities to talk with native speakers*)

PAGE 13 How is life different for college students living abroad than for high school exchange students? (*High school exchange students live with host families while college students live in buildings with other students.*)

PAGE 17 Are members of the military stationed overseas only during wartime? (*No, they are also stationed overseas in peacetime.*)

PAGE 18 How long do people serve in the Peace Corps? (*two years*)

PAGES 18–21 What are some of the types of work that Peace Corps workers do overseas? (*teach English, help people become better farmers, help protect the environment, help people start and run businesses*)

REVISIT THE BOOK

READER RESPONSE

1. Possible response: Speaking a foreign language with native speakers improves students' own skills. Exchange students may miss their families. College students who choose to study in other parts of the world usually enjoy traveling, meeting new people, and learning new customs.

2. Possible response: to work, to study, to serve in the military, to volunteer

3. Possible response: People travel a broad distance to live elsewhere.

4. Possible response: The headings clearly outlined the different reasons that people choose to live abroad.

EXTEND UNDERSTANDING Have students look through the book again, paying particular attention to the photographs. Discuss how the photos add to or take away from the meaning of the book. Have students look back at the picture on the front cover. Does that picture have new meaning now that they have read the book?

RESPONSE OPTIONS

WRITING Have students imagine that they will live abroad someday in the future. Have them pick one of the reasons in the book for living abroad. Ask them to describe where they would want to live and why. How long will they stay, and what will they do there?

SOCIAL STUDIES CONNECTION

Time For
SOCIAL
STUDIES

Have students research the Peace Corps, using the library or the Internet. Have them find out how long the organization has been in existence and how many countries it has served. How many volunteers have contributed to the program? Have them find out about some of the specific projects created by Peace Corps volunteers.

Skill Work

TEACH/REVIEW VOCABULARY

Encourage student pairs to find the vocabulary words in the text. Have them define the words and then work together to write a sentence for each word.

ELL Ask English learners to skim the story and write down any unfamiliar words. Suggest they look up the words in the dictionary and write the meaning in their notebook.

TARGET SKILL AND STRATEGY

FACT AND OPINION Remind students that a statement of *fact* is a statement that can be proven true or false; a statement of *opinion* is someone's viewpoint. Explain that facts can be proven true or false by checking in books; by observing, weighing, or measuring; or by consulting an expert. Give students several sentences, some of which are fact and some opinion, and have them label each accordingly. Then have students write their own statements of fact and statements of opinion about any topic they choose.

TEXT STRUCTURE Remind students that authors use different *text structures* to help readers pay attention to certain details about the topic. Review the headings in the text. This book is organized according to the different reasons people have for living abroad—for example, to study, to serve in the military, to volunteer.

ADDITIONAL SKILL INSTRUCTION

CAUSE AND EFFECT Remind students that an *effect* is what happened and a *cause* is why it happened. Ask: What causes people to want to live abroad? *(a desire to learn about foreign culture and language, to help others, to serve in the military)*

Fact and Opinion

When you read nonfiction, you will read some sentences that contain statements of **fact** and others that contain statements of **opinion**. Facts can be proved true or false. Opinions are statements of ideas and feelings. They cannot be proved.

Directions Read the following sentences from *Living Abroad*. Write whether each one is a fact or an opinion, and explain why.

1. High school and college students can study in other countries.

_____

2. Diplomats are government workers who represent the United States abroad.

_____

3. American students who go to school in other countries are called exchange students.

_____

4. Others may move to help people in other countries learn to live better lives.

_____

5. A member of the military sent to another country is stationed in that country.

_____

6. The Peace Corps is part of the United States government, and it sends people overseas to volunteer.

_____

7. Americans who move to other countries learn to respect and understand the differences among people of different cultures.

_____

8. Any adult can join the Peace Corps, but most volunteers are young adults.

_____

9. Anthropologists are scientists who study how other people live.

_____

10. Settling in a new place and meeting new people can spark creative ideas.

_____

Name _____

Vocabulary

Directions Fill in the blank with the word from the box that matches the definition.

Check the Words You Know

___abroad   ___ancient
___anthropologists   ___archeologists
___deployed   ___stationed
___transferred   ___volunteers

---

1. _____ *v.* having been assigned a station; placed

2. _____ *n.* people who study the people, customs, and life of ancient times

3. _____ *n.* people who work without pay

4. _____ *adv.* outside your country; to a foreign land

5. _____ *adj.* of times long past

6. _____ *v.* spread out troops into position for combat

7. _____ *n.* people who study human beings, especially fossil remains, physical characteristics, cultures, customs, and beliefs

8. _____ *v.* moved from one person or place to another

It's a World of Time Zones

SUMMARY Telling time is simple. What do you do if you want to know the time on the other side of the world? This book explains when and why time zones were invented, and how to use them to tell time around the world.

LESSON VOCABULARY

accurate	border
calculations	conference
horizon	observatory
rotation	solar time
standard	

INTRODUCE THE BOOK

INTRODUCE THE TITLE AND AUTHOR Discuss with students the title and the author of *It's a World of Time Zones*. Ask them to say what they think the book will be about based on the title and the cover illustration. Ask them to explain the meaning of the term *time zone*.

BUILD BACKGROUND Invite students to explain the reasons for night and day. *(earth's rotation on its axis)* Ask: When it's day here, what is it on the other side of the world? Why? Ask them if they have friends or family who live in a different time zone. Ask: What do you do if you want to call them on the phone? How do you know what time it is there?

PREVIEW/USE TEXT FEATURES Have students preview the book by looking at the photographs, diagrams, and maps. In particular, have them notice the chapter headings. Ask them to think about how the book is organized, based on the chapter headings. Ask how text features give an idea of what they will learn from reading this book.

READ THE BOOK

SET PURPOSE Have students set a purpose for reading *It's a World of Time Zones*. Students' interest in telling time and the history of establishing time zones around the world should guide this purpose.

STRATEGY SUPPORT: MONITOR AND FIX UP Have students use a graphic organizer to write down each point in the text where understanding breaks down. Have students ask a few questions at each of these points, such as "What happened first, next, and last?" Then have them continue reading.

COMPREHENSION QUESTIONS

PAGE 4 What are the two ways time is measured? *(by the year and by the day)*

PAGE 7 Many years ago, each place kept its own time. What happened to change the way we keep time? *(In the 1800s, railroads were built and time schedules became too complicated.)*

PAGE 9 Why was the time in the town of Greenwich, England, chosen to base time zones on? *(It had an observatory that kept accurate information on Earth's rotation.)*

PAGE 12 Why are the world's time zones often in a zigzag pattern from north to south? *(Some countries or states moved the time zone boundaries in one direction or another so that the whole country or state would be in the same time zone.)*

PAGE 12 If you are going from Atlanta to London, how many time zones will you cross? In which direction? *(five; going east)*

PAGE 17 Where is the International Date Line? *(It runs through the middle of the Pacific Ocean.)*

REVISIT THE BOOK

READER RESPONSE

1. 1) Each town sets its own time. 2) Railroads let people travel long distances quickly. 3) People divide the world into 24 time zones at a conference in Washington, D.C.

2. Read ahead because there is more explanation on the next page.

3. border; because it's a line that separates two countries

4. Denver—2:16 P.M.; Los Angeles—1:16 P.M.; New York—4:16 P.M.

EXTEND UNDERSTANDING Have students comment on the photos and maps in the selection. Invite them to explain how the visuals help support the information presented in the text. Ask: Do you think this book did a good job of visually presenting the information? What would you have added?

RESPONSE OPTIONS

WRITING Have students work in pairs to write each other postcards from different places in the world. Have them figure out what time it is in each place as they write and explain what they have been doing. Students may wish to add a picture showing this activity on the front of their postcards. Have students exchange and read the cards.

SOCIAL STUDIES CONNECTION

Time For SOCIAL STUDIES

Students can learn more about international time zones by visiting the library or using the Internet. They may wish to visit interactive sites such as http://nist.time.gov/.

Skill Work

TEACH/REVIEW VOCABULARY

To help students better remember the contextual meaning of *rotation,* have them reread page 4. Ask: What other words on this page help you understand the meaning of rotation? Continue in a similar fashion with the other vocabulary words.

ELL Invite students to use each of the vocabulary words in a sentence. Challenge them to compare terminology in English and in their home language.

TARGET SKILL AND STRATEGY

SEQUENCE Remind students that *sequence* means "order." Explain that clue words such as *first, then,* and *finally* are not always present to signal sequence. Invite them to look for other clues to sequence as they read. Clues include times of day and dates.

MONITOR AND FIX UP Remind students that a good reader knows that what they read should make sense. A good reader takes note of when he or she has lost the sense of the book. A good reader also has techniques or strategies for figuring out why understanding has broken down. She or he knows ways to figure out where understanding broke down in order to restore understanding. Challenge students to take note, as they read, of any point when they stop understanding the text. Suggest they improve their understanding by reviewing the sequence of events in that section before going on.

ADDITIONAL SKILL INSTRUCTION

DRAW CONCLUSIONS Remind students that a *conclusion* is a decision you reach that makes sense after you think about details or facts in what you read. Challenge students to think about the details and what happens in the selection as they read. Have them use a graphic organizer to jot down conclusions about the selection.

Name _____

Sequence

- **Sequence** is the order of events in a story.
- Authors sometimes use clue words such as **first, next, then,** and **last** to tell the order of events.

Directions Read the following statements from *It's a World of Time Zones*. Put the statements in the correct sequence in the graphic organizer below.

Train schedules made people think about time. People from twenty-five countries met at a conference in Washington, D.C., to solve the problem of telling time around the world. The countries at the conference decided to divide the world into twenty-four time zones. The railroads in the United States divided the country into four standard time zones.

1.

2.

3.

4.

Name _____

Vocabulary

Directions Read each sentence. Write the word from the word box that has the same meaning as the underlined word or phrase.

Check the Words You Know

___accurate   ___border   ___calculations

___conference   ___horizon   ___observatory

___rotation   ___solar time   ___standard

1. The four <u>normal</u> time zones are Eastern, Central, Mountain, and Pacific.

_____

2. At a <u>meeting</u> in Washington, D.C., 25 countries created international time zones.

_____

3. The nations of the world started with Greenwich, England, because of

its excellent <u>facility for observing the movement of planets and stars</u>.

_____

4. One day is measured by the time it takes the Earth to complete one <u>turn on its axis</u>.

_____

5. Today, when travelers cross the <u>boundary</u> separating China from Kazakhstan, they

have to set their watches ahead by four hours. _____

6. In former times, clocks and watches were not very <u>correct</u>.

_____

7. Years ago, each town kept its own time, based on <u>the time of day as figured out by</u>

<u>using the sun as a guide</u>. _____

8. Travelers who cross the International Date Line must use <u>steps for working out</u>

<u>the answers to mathematical problems</u> to figure out what time they will arrive.

_____

9. Every night, the sun sinks below the <u>western front</u>. _____

Mixing, Kneading, and Baking: The Baker's Art

3.5.4

◎ **DRAW CONCLUSIONS**
◎ **SUMMARIZE**

SUMMARY This book describes the process of baking a variety of bread products and follows a day in the life of a baker named Claudia. On this particular day, she arrives at 2:00 A.M. and bakes rosemary bread and muffins. Soon she is ready to greet her first customer of the day!

LESSON VOCABULARY

baker's dozen	bakery
carbon dioxide	dough
fermentation	ingredients
knead	professional
recipe	yeast

INTRODUCE THE BOOK

INTRODUCE THE TITLE AND AUTHOR Discuss with students the title and author of *Mixing, Kneading, and Baking: The Baker's Art.* Ask students what they think the book will be about. Do they think baking could be considered an art?

BUILD BACKGROUND Discuss students' interest in baking. Ask if any of them have ever baked bread or watched bread being made. Have them describe the process.

PREVIEW/USE TEXT FEATURES Encourage students to look at the captions, photos, charts, and the map on page 19. How many of the international breads listed on page 19 have they eaten?

READ THE BOOK

SET PURPOSE Have students set a purpose for reading *Mixing, Kneading, and Baking: The Baker's Art.* Remind students that setting a purpose helps guide their reading. They could think about the science of baking, or a particular baked good that they enjoy.

STRATEGY SUPPORT: SUMMARIZE Draw students' attention to the two tables on pages 6 and 11. Point out that tables are graphic ways of organizing lists or steps. Students may want to make their own lists as they read. Alternatively, they can summarize the details for a section after reading it. Remind students that a good summary leaves out unimportant details.

COMPREHENSION QUESTIONS

PAGE 4 What would happen if Claudia got to work at 4:00 A.M. instead of 2:00 A.M.? *(She would be late getting started baking and wouldn't be ready to serve her customers.)*

PAGE 5 Why do bakers wear white? *(to keep the food clean)*

PAGE 6 Why do bakers use such large ovens? *(They have many things to bake at the same time.)*

PAGES 8–17 Summarize the tasks that Claudia must complete before her bakery opens. *(gets out ingredients and weighs them, makes rosemary bread, makes muffins, gets the cash register ready)*

PAGE 13 What are the names of some of the different shapes of bread? *(boule or ball, batard or torpedo, fendu or split loaf, braided loaf)*

REVISIT THE BOOK

READER RESPONSE

1. Possible response: The dough wouldn't rise.
2. Responses should give an overview of the steps listed in the chart on page 11.
3. Possible response: Bakery in center; in surrounding ovals: oven; kitchen; recipe; bread; rolls; cakes
4. Possible response: China: mooncake; Germany: pretzel; Russia: pumpernickel; Italy: focaccia

EXTEND UNDERSTANDING Have students examine the table on page 11. Ask: Is this a helpful way to list the various steps needed to bake bread? Then have students find a recipe for baking bread in a cookbook or online. Do they think they could bake bread by following that recipe?

RESPONSE OPTIONS

WRITING Have students imagine they are bakers. If they arrived at their bakery for work at 2:00 A.M., what would they bake first for their customers?

SOCIAL STUDIES CONNECTION

Time For SOCIAL STUDIES

Have students research chocolate on the Internet or using library resources. What is the history of cocoa? What are its cooking and baking properties? What countries grow cocoa beans and which countries are known for producing the finest chocolate?

Skill Work

TEACH/REVIEW VOCABULARY

Review the vocabulary words with students. What can students learn about baking from knowing the definitions of *yeast, carbon dioxide,* and *fermentation*? *(When yeast is added to dough, it eats the sugars in the dough, producing carbon dioxide, which causes the dough to rise.)*

ELL Have students describe the types of bread eaten in their home country. Have them describe the process for making bread there.

TARGET SKILL AND STRATEGY

DRAW CONCLUSIONS Remind students that to *draw a conclusion* means making a decision that makes sense after thinking about facts or details. Have students think about the following question as they read: Why does a baker need to start work so early in the morning? *(to have fresh baked goods ready to be sold first thing in the morning)*

SUMMARIZE Remind students that *summarizing* is boiling down a story to its main points. To gain practice, have students summarize their favorite books or movies. They can also take notes on the baking process as they read, and summarize the process upon finishing reading the book.

ADDITIONAL SKILL INSTRUCTION

MAIN IDEA Remind students that most stories have one or more *main ideas*. Ask students to take notes as they read, listing the main points and supporting details. Ask: What is the most important thing a baker does each day?

Draw Conclusions

- To draw a **conclusion** is to think about facts and details and decide something about them.

Directions Read the following passage from *Mixing, Kneading, and Baking: The Baker's Art.* Then write two facts about yeast and draw a conclusion.

> Yeast is a tiny, live organism. It eats the sugars that are part of the dough. As it does, the yeast gives off a gas called carbon dioxide. The gas causes the dough to expand. This process is called fermentation. This process makes the bread soft and chewy.

1. Fact: _____

2. Fact: _____

3. Conclusion: _____

Directions Read the following passage from *Mixing, Kneading, and Baking: The Baker's Art.* Then write two facts about Lisa on the lines below. See what conclusion you can draw.

> When Lisa comes in and orders twelve muffins, Claudia gives her an extra one for free. That's called a baker's dozen.

4. Fact: _____

5. Fact: _____

6. Conclusion: _____

Vocabulary

Directions Complete each sentence with the word from the box that fits best.

Check the Words You Know

___baker's dozen   ___bakery
___carbon dioxide   ___dough
___fermentation   ___ingredients
___knead   ___professional
___recipe   ___yeast

1. When yeast is added to dough, _____ is produced.

2. The baker refused to give out her _____ for raisin bread.

3. Before beginning, the baker set out all of the _____ he would need.

4. Claudia's favorite step in the recipe was shaping the _____ .

5. The process of fermentation began after the _____ was added to the dough.

6. When Lisa ordered a dozen muffins, she got thirteen, or a

_____ .

7. Although it can be tiring work, Claudia loves to _____ the dough.

8. The chef at the restaurant is talented and _____ .

9. When yeast consumes sugars in dough, the process of _____ takes place.

10. To buy the freshest bread, go to your neighborhood _____ early in the morning.

Let's Go Have Fun!

SUMMARY This nonfiction text explores various places to have fun. However, the information is purveyed by a fictitious character, a teacher named Mrs. Garcia. Students will learn more specific details about topics that are probably already familiar, such as skateboarding and national parks.

LESSON VOCABULARY

acrobatics   championship
exhibits   geysers
interactive   recreation
spectacular

INTRODUCE THE BOOK

INTRODUCE THE TITLE AND AUTHOR Introduce students to the title and author of the book *Let's Go Have Fun!* Ask students what kind of information they think the book will provide based on its title. Also ask students what clues are available in the cover photograph.

BUILD BACKGROUND Ask students if they have ever gone to a state fair, and if so, what they remember about it. Also ask students if they have ever been to a national park and what they saw there. Then tell students that by reading this book, they will learn more about state fairs, national parks, and many other ways to have fun.

ELL Invite students to share a personal experience involving going someplace special to have fun. Suggest sporting events, circuses, and fairs, but explain that students do not have to limit their responses to those places.

PREVIEW/USE TEXT FEATURES Suggest that students skim the text and pay close attention to the photos and illustrations. Ask them what clues these visual elements give regarding what the book might be about.

READ THE BOOK

SET PURPOSE Encourage students to set a purpose for reading this book. Have students discuss what they would like to learn from this text based on their preview and the background discussions. They may be interested in one of the activities or places mentioned in the book. Ask them to write down two questions that they hope the book will answer.

STRATEGY SUPPORT: PRIOR KNOWLEDGE If students have prior knowledge of an activity or place mentioned in *Let's Go Have Fun!,* they are more likely to be interested in and comprehend the new material presented in the book.

COMPREHENSION QUESTIONS

PAGE 5 Is the following sentence a fact or an opinion? You can spend the whole day and night at the fair and never get bored. *(opinion)*

PAGE 7 Name four things that began at state fairs. *(cotton candy, corn dogs, butter sculptures, microwave ovens)*

PAGES 8–9 List three facts about the famous geyser, Old Faithful. *(Possible responses: It erupts about every 76 minutes. It shoots thousands of gallons of boiling water. It is in Yellowstone National Park.)*

PAGE 10 What is your favorite sport or other kind of recreation? Why? *(Responses will vary.)*

PAGE 24 Write a sentence using two of the vocabulary words. *(Possible response: A spectacular goal was made at the hockey state championship.)*

REVIST THE BOOK

READER RESPONSE

1. to inform the reader that there are many ways to have fun, no matter where you live
2. Possible responses: Learned About: state fair, national park, Little League, skateboarding. Favorites: parties, family reunions, soccer, making jewelry
3. Possible responses: For recreation today, we went to the museum. The exhibit was spectacular.
4. Possible responses: Old Faithful is a geyser that erupts about every 76 minutes.

EXTEND UNDERSTANDING Invite students to look at the map on pages 8 and 9. Explain that maps are one type of visual aid that can help readers understand information in a text. Ask: In what part of the United States are most canyons found? (west) Where is the northernmost park on the map? (Maine) the southernmost? (Florida)

RESPONSE OPTIONS

WRITING Ask students to look at the map on pages 8 and 9. Then ask them to choose one national park from the map that they would like to visit someday. Have students use the Internet to do research about a state park and then write a paragraph about the features of that park.

SCIENCE CONNECTION

TIME FOR Science

Geysers such as Old Faithful are unusual and fascinating natural features. Invite students to do research on the Internet or in the library to find out what makes geysers shoot hot water and steam. Ask students to find out how geysers are different from volcanoes.

Skill Work

TEACH/REVIEW VOCABULARY

Invite students to look up the vocabulary words in the Glossary. Then ask them to write a paragraph using any two of the words. Encourage students to write about their own personal experiences or to create a fictional story.

TARGET SKILL AND STRATEGY

AUTHOR'S PURPOSE Remind students that the author's purpose is the reason why the author wrote the book, and that it can be to inform, entertain, persuade, or express a mood or feeling. Invite students to discuss why they think the author wrote *Let's Go Have Fun!* Then ask students if they think the author wanted to inform and entertain.

PRIOR KNOWLEDGE Remind students that prior knowledge gathered from other books or their personal experiences can help them understand a book. Ask students if any of them have raised farm animals, skateboarded, or played on a Little League team. Have those students explain something about their activity that the other students may not know—for example, how much a horse eats or how many people are needed to make a baseball team.

ADDITIONAL SKILL INSTRUCTION

COMPARE AND CONTRAST Remind students that a comparison tells how two or more things are alike and different, and a contrast shows how two or more things are different. Words such as *like* and *as* can be clues that an author is making comparisons. Clue words such as *but* and *unlike* show that an author is making contrasts. Explain that clue words are not always used. Encourage students to ask compare/contrast questions such as "How are state fairs and Little League alike and different?" as they read this work.

Author's Purpose

- The **author's purpose** is the reason or reasons an author has for writing a story.
- An author may have one or more reasons for writing. He or she may want to **inform, persuade, entertain,** or **express** a mood or feeling.

Directions Read the following passage. Then answer the questions below.

Skateboarding is no longer what it once was. Long ago, skateboards were homemade, with roller-skate wheels attached to a plank of wood.

Now skateboarding is an entirely different ballgame! Skateboarders perform moves called *ollies, McTwists,* and *caballerials.* Watch as the skater flips, spins, and turns, and you'll see gravity at work. Gravity holds the skateboard in place with the force of nature.

1. Why do you think the author wrote this paragraph?

   _____

   _____

2. Write a fact from the paragraph that gives information about skateboarding.

   _____

   _____

3. Write a fact from the paragraph about skateboarders.

   _____

   _____

4. Do you think the author had more than one reason for writing about skateboards?

   Why do you think this?

   _____

   _____

5. Why do you think the author explains to the reader about gravity?

   _____

   _____

© Pearson Education 3

Vocabulary

Directions Fill in each blank with the word from the word box that best fits the definition.

Check the Words You Know

__acrobatics __championship __exhibits __geysers
__interactive __recreation __spectacular

1. underground springs that spew steam from the earth _____

2. impressive or dramatic to watch _____

3. the final stage of a sports tournament or competition _____

4. the skills or performance routines of an acrobat _____

5. allowing the exchange of information between a person and a machine

_____

6. displays of objects of interest, especially in museums _____

7. an activity that a person does for fun _____

Directions Write a paragraph about state fairs. Use as many vocabulary words as possible.

_____

_____

_____

_____

French Roots in North America

SUMMARY This book gives students facts about visiting places in North America that were once ruled by France. It shows how French culture can still be found in those places.

LESSON VOCABULARY

assembly line	bilingual
descendants	echo chamber
fortified	immigrants
influence	strait

INTRODUCE THE BOOK

INTRODUCE THE TITLE AND AUTHOR Discuss with students the title and the author of *French Roots in North America*. Ask students what they imagine this reading selection will be about, based on the title. Invite students to look at the cover illustration and discuss how this gives them more information about the selection.

BUILD BACKGROUND Discuss with students what they know about France and French culture.

ELL Invite students to discuss the parts of their cultures that they find in America, and what parts of other cultures are still in their native countries.

PREVIEW/USE ILLUSTRATIONS Suggest students glance through the photographs and illustrations in the reading selection. Ask students which images are familiar to them and which are not. Point out the chapter headings and ask students how these help them understand what they are going to be reading about. Ask students how the photos with captioned text give the selection the flavor of someone's travel journal.

READ THE BOOK

SET PURPOSE Have students set a purpose for reading *French Roots in North America*. Students' interest in geography and how foreign countries influence the United States should help guide this purpose.

STRATEGY SUPPORT: TEXT STRUCTURE Remind students that the *text structure* describes and defines different cities that still have French culture. Suggest that as students read *French Roots in North America*, they use a graphic organizer to list each visited city and the descriptions about each city.

COMPREHENSION QUESTIONS

PAGE 4 How did the author record her trip? What does each different recording method add to the story? *(journal writing: tells us the narrator's inner thoughts; video and postcards: give visuals and descriptions; interviews: give someone else's thoughts on the subject)*

PAGE 8 What is the main point of the paragraph about Detroit? *(Antoine de la Mothe Cadillac started a settlement called Fort Pontchartrain du Détroit.)*

PAGE 9 Why do you think the author used a series of photographs and captions in the text structure? *(The photos make it look realistic.)*

REVISIT THE BOOK

READER RESPONSE

1. Main idea: There is still much of the old French culture throughout North America. Details and sentence will vary.

2. The chapter titles point out the topic of each section and the names of the places visited. They get me ready to read more about them.

3. *Influence* can be used as a verb and it means "to convince." Sentence: What we read *influences* our thinking.

4. Elements of French culture: Quebec City: people still speak French and English; Detroit: many streets still have French names; New Orleans: has a French colonial center and Mardi Gras celebration comes from the French; St. Louis: a French name; St. Lucia: has French music, language, and food

EXTEND UNDERSTANDING Direct students' attention to the narrator, or the person who is telling the story. Ask students how the selection might have been different if there were no narrator, but just a series of facts presented instead.

RESPONSE OPTIONS

WRITING Invite students to write their own postcards from two or more of the places mentioned in the text.

SOCIAL STUDIES CONNECTION

Time For SOCIAL STUDIES

Suggest students further research one of the places mentioned in the book. Then invite students to write and illustrate a travel brochure encouraging people to visit that place.

Skill Work

TEACH/REVIEW VOCABULARY

Review vocabulary words with students. Give students sentences with vocabulary words used correctly and incorrectly. Have students tell you whether the sentence is "true" or "false." Encourage students to correct the "false" sentences so the vocabulary word used makes sense.

TARGET SKILL AND STRATEGY

MAIN IDEA Remind students that the *main idea* is the most important idea about a topic. It can be expressed in one sentence at the beginning, middle, or end of the selection. Sometimes, however, students must put it into their own words. Remind students that as they read, they should try to pick out the main idea and write down details that support their answer.

TEXT STRUCTURE Remind students that *text structure* is the way a text is organized. Explain that the structure of this selection includes description and definition. Remind students that understanding internal text structure can help them to pick out the main idea. Suggest they take notes as they read, listing the descriptions of each city and the type of text structure used to describe each city.

ADDITIONAL SKILL INSTRUCTION

FACT AND OPINION Remind students that a *statement of fact* is something that can be proven or disproven. A *statement of opinion* is someone's beliefs and cannot be proven. It often includes clue words such as *I believe* or *in my opinion*. Remind students that a sentence can include both a statement of fact and a statement of opinion. Remind students to try to pick out statements of fact and statements of opinion as they read *French Roots in North America*.

Main Idea

- The **main idea** is the most important idea about a reading selection.
- Sometimes it is stated at the beginning, middle, or end of the selection; but sometimes it isn't and you must figure it out yourself.

Directions Below are groups of three sentences. Write *M* next to the sentence that is the main idea and *D* next to the sentences that are the supporting details.

_____ **1.** No trip to Detroit is complete without a visit to the Henry Ford car museum.

_____ **2.** Because of the automobile industry, Detroit is called Motor City.

_____ **3.** Detroit is the home of the automobile industry.

_____ **4.** In the 1820s, the French fur-trading families began to lose their influence.

_____ **5.** The first major in the local army was an English-speaking doctor.

_____ **6.** The population grew to include Germans, Irish, and others.

_____ **7.** The strongest tradition in St. Lucia is African, but there is a large amount of French culture.

_____ **8.** French is still spoken in St. Lucia.

_____ **9.** There is a great deal of French music in St. Lucia.

10. What was the main idea of *French Roots in North America?*

_____

_____

Name _____

Vocabulary

Directions Unscramble the vocabulary words. Write the letter of the correct definition on the line.

Check the Words You Know

___assembly line	___bilingual	___descendants	___echo chamber
___fortified	___immigrants	___influences	___strait

_____ **1.** gualbiiln _____

_____ **2.** mmgistnari _____

_____ **3.** stiart _____

_____ **4.** fluinensec _____

_____ **5.** blyssaem enli _____

_____ **6.** roftideif _____

_____ **7.** hoec hamcber _____

_____ **8.** cendesdants _____

a. what you are if you speak two languages

b. things that have effects on someone or something

c. a narrow strip of water that connects two larger bodies of water

d. people who leave one country and settle in another

e. room or space with walls that reflect sound so that an echo is made

f. made stronger against attack

g. in a factory, work passing from one person or machine to the next

h. people who are related to someone who lived in the past

China's Gifts to the World

SUMMARY This book describes the art and culture of China. It focuses on the ancient art of calligraphy, describing the process by which calligraphers make their own ink and study how to make the 50,000 characters in the Chinese written language.

LESSON VOCABULARY

bristles	dialects
diverse	expedition
flourished	ingredient
inspiration	literate
muffled	techniques
translation	

INTRODUCE THE BOOK

INTRODUCE THE TITLE AND AUTHOR Introduce students to the title and the author of the book. Ask students what kind of information they think this book will provide, based on the title.

BUILD BACKGROUND Discuss with students what they know about China. What do they know about the art of calligraphy? Ask students if they ever studied an art form (music, drawing) that required lots of practice.

PREVIEW/USE ILLUSTRATIONS AND CAPTIONS Suggest students skim the text and look at the illustrations and captions. Ask students what clues these elements give them as to what this book might be about.

ELL Ask students to look at the historical map on page 4. Have them trace the trade routes and identify the countries that the routes passed through.

READ THE BOOK

SET PURPOSE Have students set a purpose for reading *China's Gifts to the World*. Students' interest and curiosity about China and the Chinese language can guide this purpose. As students read, suggest that they take down notes that might provide answers to any questions they have about the subject.

STRATEGY SUPPORT: GRAPHIC ORGANIZERS To give students more support in learning to summarize and organize what they read, help them apply a graphic organizer to reading this book. For instance, draw attention to the chart on page 23. Ask students how it helps to make the Chinese character clear.

COMPREHENSION QUESTIONS

PAGE 5 How was China kept isolated from the rest of the world for so many years? *(It is surrounded by tall mountains and huge deserts.)*

PAGE 11 Read the poem by Li Po. What feeling does this poem give you? *(peaceful, calm, happy)*

PAGE 15 Look at the table. Why is it important to make all the ink you will need at one time? *(It is difficult to make two batches of ink that are exactly the same color.)*

PAGE 17 Do you think it takes longer to learn our 26-letter alphabet, or 7,000 Chinese characters? *(longer to learn the Chinese characters since they need more practice)*

REVISIT THE BOOK

READER RESPONSE

1. The language is written in pictures instead of letters.
2. brushes; ink sticks; ink stones; paper
3. Antonyms: *diverse,* same; *flourished,* fared poorly; *literate,* illiterate, not able to read or write, uneducated; *muffled,* clear, sharp
4. practicing to use a brush ("mo"); copying from a model ("lin"); writing your own thoughts and developing your own style ("xie") Responses will vary.

EXTEND UNDERSTANDING Have students research the history of our alphabet on the Internet. Can they easily read a book that was first printed in 1600? Have them imagine what it would be like to live in China and be easily able to read poems and books printed at that time.

RESPONSE OPTIONS

WRITING Imagine that you are traveling to China with the young Marco Polo in the late 1200s. Describe the things that you see, smell, and taste along the way. Describe what it is like to see Chinese writing for the first time.

SOCIAL STUDIES CONNECTION

Time For SOCIAL STUDIES

There were many things that the Chinese developed before the Europeans. Make a list of some of the things that the book says were first invented in China.

Skill Work

TEACH/REVIEW VOCABULARY

To reinforce the contextual meaning of the word *literate* on page 6, discuss with students how the phrase *can read* helps to guess the meaning of the world *literate.* Do this with the rest of the vocabulary words in the story.

TARGET SKILL AND STRATEGY

CAUSE AND EFFECT Remind students that an *effect* is what happened, and a *cause* is why something happened. Have the students read pages 9–10. Ask: Why was the poet Li Po sent to jail?

GRAPHIC ORGANIZERS Remind students that *graphic organizers* are visual ways to organize information as they read. Students can use graphic organizers to strengthen their understanding of the text. Have the students create a cause-and-effect chart and fill it in as they read whenever they come to an event or happening that was caused by another event.

ADDITIONAL SKILL INSTRUCTION

GENERALIZE Remind students that a *generalization* is a broad statement or rule that applies to many examples. Have students read about brushes on page 12. While the text describes some of the different kinds of brushes, what elements are common to all brushes? *(bamboo reed handle, animal hair bristles)*

Name _____

Cause and Effect

- A **cause** is why something happened.
- An **effect** is what happened.

Directions Skim through *China's Gifts to the World* to find the text on the following topics. For each topic, list one cause and one effect.

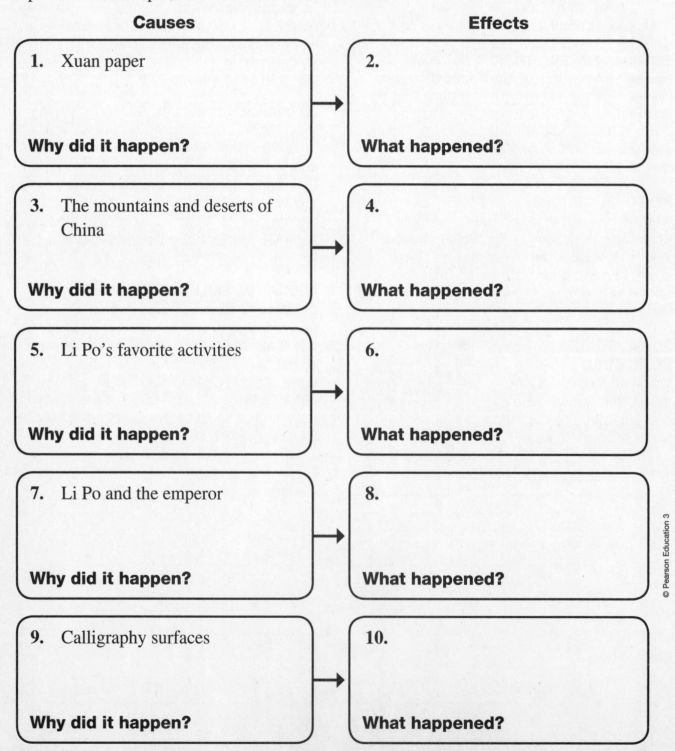

Causes	Effects
1. Xuan paper **Why did it happen?**	**2.** **What happened?**
3. The mountains and deserts of China **Why did it happen?**	**4.** **What happened?**
5. Li Po's favorite activities **Why did it happen?**	**6.** **What happened?**
7. Li Po and the emperor **Why did it happen?**	**8.** **What happened?**
9. Calligraphy surfaces **Why did it happen?**	**10.** **What happened?**

Name _____

Vocabulary

Directions Fill in the blank with the word from the box that matches the definition.

Check the Words You Know

___ bristles   ___ dialects   ___ diverse
___ expedition   ___ flourished   ___ ingredient
___ inspiration   ___ literate   ___ muffled
___ techniques   ___ translation

1. _____ *v.* steadily grew, expanded

2. _____ *n.* something that stimulates a person to be creative

3. _____ *n.* the hairs on a brush

4. _____ *adj.* unable to be heard; wrapped with material to deaden the sound

5. _____ *n.* one of several substances mixed together to make a new substance

6. _____ *n.* a journey with a specific purpose

7. _____ *n.* methods of doing something

Directions Write a paragraph about China using the words *dialects, diverse, literate,* and *translation.*

_____

_____

_____

_____

_____

_____

_____

The Huge Paintings of Thomas Hart Benton

🌀 **FACT AND OPINION**
🌀 **MONITOR AND FIX UP**

SUMMARY This is a biography of American muralist Thomas Hart Benton. It supports the lesson concept of freedom of expression in a free society.

LESSON VOCABULARY

ally	appreciated
encouraged	enlisted
expression	legacy
murals	native
social	support

INTRODUCE THE BOOK

INTRODUCE THE TITLE AND AUTHOR Discuss with students the title and the author of *The Huge Paintings of Thomas Hart Benton*. Explain that the book is a biography, or the real story of someone's life. Ask students to name other biographies they may have read.

BUILD BACKGROUND Discuss what students know about murals. If they have ever seen a public mural or helped create a mural, have them share their experiences.

PREVIEW/USE TEXT FEATURES Ask students to look at the table of contents. Discuss how it helps them to easily locate information in the book. Also discuss with students why each photo and art reproduction has a caption. Ask: How do the captions add to your understanding of the images and text?

READ THE BOOK

SET PURPOSE Have students set a purpose for reading *The Huge Paintings of Thomas Hart Benton*. Ask students to consider the chapter titles they read in their preview. Help students by asking them to complete this sentence: I wonder _____.

STRATEGY SUPPORT: MONITOR AND FIX UP Remind students that as they read a story, they should monitor, or check, their understanding of what they are reading. Tell students that one way to check is to ask questions. Model important questions that students should ask themselves as they read nonfiction: "What is the author trying to tell us? What does this mean? Does this make sense? Do I understand this?" Remind students that if they can't answer the questions, they should use a fix-up strategy like reread and review or skim and scan. To help students use the strategy while they read, suggest that each time students complete a chapter, they write a question about the chapter and try to answer it.

COMPREHENSION QUESTIONS

PAGE 5 Read the sentence, *Every school should have them.* Is it a statement of fact or a statement of opinion? Why? *(It is a statement of opinion, because it cannot be proved true or false.)*

PAGES 6–7 Do you think Benton's early childhood affected his later work as an artist? Why or why not? *(Possible response: Yes, he met many of the kinds of people he painted later in life.)*

PAGES 16–17 Why did the author include the story about Benton and President Truman? *(to inform and entertain)*

PAGE 19 Do you like Benton's paintings? Why or why not? *(Possible response: I like them because they are very colorful and lively.)*

REVISIT THE BOOK

READER RESPONSE

1. Possible responses: Fact: People traveled by steamship and train. People aboard riverboats enjoyed music and dancing. Opinion: Travel aboard a riverboat was more fun than travel aboard a train. Dance steps and movements were strange.

2. He wanted to make very large pieces of artwork. He needed a lot of space to get his ideas across.

3. Other definitions: living or liking to live with others; liking company; connected with fashionable society. Sentences will vary.

4. Responses will vary.

EXTEND UNDERSTANDING Ask students to choose three photo or art reproduction captions. Have them explain the information each caption provides that is not available from viewing the photo alone.

RESPONSE OPTIONS

WRITING Have students write a paragraph that compares the relative merits of the work of Benton and Picasso.

SOCIAL STUDIES CONNECTION

Time For SOCIAL STUDIES

Explain to students that Benton was one of many artists employed under New Deal art programs during the Great Depression. Have students conduct research about these programs and how they helped artists and society in general. Have them share their findings in small groups.

Skill Work

TEACH/REVIEW VOCABULARY

Form student pairs. Have each partner write a cloze sentence for a vocabulary word. Ask them to exchange sentences and fill in the correct word. Have students repeat the activity until all the words have been used.

ELL Make one set of cards for the vocabulary words and another set for their definitions. Have students play a memory game by pairing words and definitions.

TARGET SKILL AND STRATEGY

FACT AND OPINION Remind students that a *statement of fact* tells something that can be proved true or false. A *statement of opinion* tells your ideas or feelings. It cannot be proved true or false. Explain that some words are clues to statements of opinion. Words such as *I believe* or *I think* and *beautiful* or *best* often signal an opinion. Have students read this statement on page 5: *He painted western rodeos.* Ask: Can you prove this statement true or false? How?

MONITOR AND FIX UP Tell students to check their understanding as they read by answering questions, such as: *What does this mean?* Remind students that if they ask and answer questions as they read, they will be able to tell the difference between a statement of fact and a statement of opinion.

ADDITIONAL SKILL INSTRUCTION

AUTHOR'S PURPOSE Remind students that the *author's purpose* means the author's reasons for writing as he or she has. Tell students that authors often have more than one reason for writing, and that to persuade, inform, express, and entertain are common reasons. As students preview the book, ask: Why do you think the author wrote this book? *(to inform and to entertain)*

Fact and Opinion

- A statement of **fact** is a statement that can be proved true or false.
- A statement of **opinion** is a statement of someone's judgment, belief, or way of thinking about something.

Directions Write *F* beside statements of fact and *O* beside statements of opinion. Then explain what makes the statement a fact or an opinion.

_____ **1.** Thomas Hart Benton is a famous muralist.

_____

_____

_____ **2.** Thomas Hart Benton is the best of the American muralists.

_____

_____

_____ **3.** His father wanted his son to go into politics.

_____

_____

_____ **4.** Art institutes are better schools than military institutes.

_____

_____

_____ **5.** New York City is the best place for an artist to live.

_____

_____

Vocabulary

Directions Draw a line from the word to its meaning.

Check the Words You Know

___ally   ___appreciate   ___encouraged   ___enlisted
___expression   ___legacy   ___mural   ___native
___social   ___support

1. ally   *n.* a local resident

2. appreciate   *n.* example, illustration, or demonstration

3. enlisted   *n.* backing, encouragement, help

4. encouraged   *n.* a friend or helper

5. expression   *v.* gave support to

6. legacy   *n.* a large wall painting

7. mural   *n.* a gift left by someone

8. native   *v.* to be grateful for

9. social   *v.* joined or signed on

10. support   *adj.* relating to human society

Directions Using at least two of the vocabulary words above, write one statement of fact and one statement of opinion.

_____

_____

_____

_____

_____

_____

A Fantastic Field Trip

SUMMARY In this science fiction story, a group of nine year olds visits a special zoo for giant bugs. While they are at the zoo they see butterflies the size of small cars, fleas that can jump more than 150 feet, and a wasps' nest as big as a garage.

LESSON VOCABULARY

announcement	budge
entomological	exhibition
expenses	nuisances

INTRODUCE THE BOOK

INTRODUCE THE TITLE AND AUTHOR Discuss the title and the author of *A Fantastic Field Trip.* Ask students about other science fiction books they may have read. What do they think may happen in this story, based on the title?

BUILD BACKGROUND Discuss with students what they know about insects, especially butterflies. Have students ever watched a butterfly emerge from a cocoon? Have they ever collected butterflies or other insects? What is the difference between a moth and a butterfly? Have any students caught fireflies?

PREVIEW/USE ILLUSTRATIONS Invite students to look at all of the illustrations in the book. Ask students to predict what will happen from looking at the pictures. Discuss which illustrations seem realistic and which seem like fantasy.

READ THE BOOK

SET PURPOSE Have students set a purpose for reading *A Fantastic Field Trip.* They may wish to identify the fantasy elements in the story, take notes on the sequence of events, or learn more about insects.

STRATEGY SUPPORT: VISUALIZE Tell students that they should combine what they already know with details from the text to create pictures in their minds about what is happening in the story. Add that they can use all of their senses, not just sight, to help put themselves in the story, increasing their enjoyment of what they read. Model: "On page 7, I read that Mrs. Appleby was stuck in traffic. I know what that's like. It's noisy, smelly, and people are impatient. I think Mrs. Appleby was worried and frustrated." After page 18, ask: What details in the story help you picture what it was like to be in the cicada exhibit?

COMPREHENSION QUESTIONS

PAGE 5 Who paid for the students' trip to the entomological zoo? *(The students raised their own money.)*

PAGE 7 Why was Mrs. Appleby late for the trip? *(She had been stuck in traffic.)*

PAGE 13 Where were the insects kept? *(in underground halls)*

PAGE 14 As the butterflies flew bush to bush, what happened? *(The wings sent gusts of wind that nearly blew the Bug Kids off their feet.)*

PAGE 15 Name a few of the moths and butterflies the kids saw. *(monarchs, spotted tiger moths, and pale cabbage moths)*

PAGE 18 Why were the wasps carrying food to the workers in the nest? *(to feed the larvae)*

REVISIT THE BOOK

READER RESPONSE

1. Possible responses: giant butterflies, pupas as big as soccer balls, the loud sounds of the insects, fleas that could jump more than 150 feet, giant ladybugs
2. Possible response: thousands of lightning bugs
3. Possible response: The story says that the entomological zoo is a place all about bugs.
4. Possible responses: I saw giant insects, fleas that could jump more than 150 feet, and thousands of lightning bugs.

EXTEND UNDERSTANDING Have students think about what elements of this story make it fantasy or science fiction. Have them list details from the story that describe things that could not really happen.

RESPONSE OPTIONS

WRITING Have students imagine that they found a giant butterfly in their backyard. What would they do with it? Have students imagine they could fly on the back of the butterfly. Where would they go, and what would they see?

SCIENCE CONNECTION

Have students research as much as they can find out about butterflies. Assign each student a different butterfly. They can use the Internet or the library. Have them draw a picture of their butterfly. Once they have gathered all their information, have them share it with the class.

Skill Work

TEACH/REVIEW VOCABULARY

Encourage student pairs to find the vocabulary words in the text. Have them define the words and then work together to write a sentence for each word.

ELL Have students describe their favorite insects. How do insects in their home countries differ from insects in this country?

TARGET SKILL AND STRATEGY

PLOT AND THEME Remind students that the *plot* is the events in a story from the beginning to the middle to the end. Also, remind students that stories usually have one big idea, or *theme*. Discuss with students what they think the big idea is of familiar stories such as "The Tortoise and the Hare" (slow and steady wins the race). Have them tell the plot of the story by recalling the events in sequence.

VISUALIZE Remind students that when we *visualize*, we form pictures in our minds about what is happening in the story. Encourage students to try to visualize the scenes and characters in *A Fantastic Field Trip* as they read it. Have them try to activate all their senses: sight, smell, taste, touch, and hearing.

ADDITIONAL SKILL INSTRUCTION

REALISM AND FANTASY Remind students that a *realistic* story tells about something that could happen. Remind them that a *fantasy* is a story about something that could not happen. As they read this story, have them think about which elements of the story are realistic and which are fantasy.

Plot and Theme

- The **plot** is an organized pattern of events.
- The **theme** is the "big idea" of a story.

Directions Fill in the table below, which will guide you through a summary of the plot and end with your naming the theme of *A Fantastic Field Trip*.

1. Title _____

2. This story is about _____

_____
(name the characters)

_____

3. This story takes place _____

_____
(where and when)

4. The action begins when _____

_____

_____

5. Then _____

_____

_____

6. Next, _____

_____

7. After that, _____

_____

8. The story ends when _____

_____

9. Theme: _____

126

© Pearson Education 3

Vocabulary

Directions Fill in the blank with the word from the box that fits best.

Check the Words You Know
___announcement   ___budge   ___entomological
___exhibition   ___expenses   ___nuisances

1. We heard the _____ that blared "Put on your sunglasses!"

2. The _____ zoo was a place that was all about bugs.

3. The Bug Kids raised money to pay for their trip's _____.

4. They tried to open the door but it wouldn't _____.

5. The entomological _____ housed many gigantic insects.

6. Although insects can be fascinating, some of them can be _____.

Directions Write a brief paragraph discussing the Bug Kids' trip to the Entomological Zoo, using as many vocabulary words as possible.

_____

_____

_____

_____

_____

_____

_____

_____

Jackie Robinson

SUMMARY Learn about the struggles African Americans faced under the laws of segregation through the achievements of Jackie Robinson. The introduction prepares the reader to predict the difficulties Jackie encountered throughout his life, while photographs help the reader visualize the time period.

LESSON VOCABULARY

adversity	descending	discrimination
guise	legacy	scholarships
segregated	sharecropper	strike

INTRODUCE THE BOOK

INTRODUCE THE TITLE AND AUTHOR Discuss with students the title and the author of *Jackie Robinson*. Encourage students to comment on what the photo on the cover tells them about Jackie. Ask students to predict what social studies topics may be discussed in this book.

BUILD BACKGROUND To help students appreciate Jackie Robinson's achievements, discuss the discrimination African Americans faced before and during the Civil Rights Movement. Clarify the meaning of the phrase *civil rights*.

ELL Build background and vocabulary by discussing the game of baseball. Explain the difference between the minor and major league teams. Discuss the popularity of the Brooklyn Dodgers and the famous athletes on that team.

PREVIEW/USE TEXT FEATURES Prompt students to look at the table of contents. Ask students how they think the information about the book is organized. As they look at the photographs, captions, and headings, guide them to use the photographs to visualize what the time period was like.

READ THE BOOK

SET PURPOSE Students who are interested in sports will be curious to read about Jackie Robinson. They may also be interested in comparing the achievements and character of their favorite athlete of today with Jackie. Other students may wish to compare everyday life of today to the everyday life under the laws of segregation.

STRATEGY SUPPORT: PREDICT/CONFIRM PREDICTIONS Encourage students to pause while reading and *predict* what will happen next. It is a good way to check comprehension. Practice this skill after students have read page 18. Ask students to predict what people will remember most about Jackie's achievements and character. After students have read page 20, discuss which predictions were correct or incorrect and why.

COMPREHENSION QUESTIONS

PAGE 7 What general statement can you make about Jackie's childhood? *(It was difficult.)*

PAGE 10 Why did Jackie believe that a college degree would not help him get a good job? *(African Americans did not have many economic choices even if they had a college degree.)*

PAGE 12 How did Branch Rickey help break the color barrier in major league baseball? *(He scouted for talented African American athletes to join his team.)*

PAGE 17 What character trait did Jackie show by standing firm and not reacting to his attackers? *(He showed self-discipline.)*

PAGE 20 What did Jackie mean when he said "A life is not important except for the impact it has on other lives"? *(People should choose to live their lives by helping others.)*

REVISIT THE BOOK

READER RESPONSE

1. Possible responses: They did not have contracts, were forced to work for lower wages, and were restricted in terms of where they could eat and sleep on the road.
2. Possible response: Baseball might not have become integrated for a long time.
3. Possible response: by adding the suffix *-tion* to make the words *discrimination* and *segregation.* Additional responses will vary.
4. Possible responses:

Event	Date
Born	1919
Left army	1944
First major league game	1947
Died	1972

EXTEND UNDERSTANDING On the bottom of page 8, the author included information about Jackie's older brother, Mack. Ask students why the author chose to have the information set apart from the other text. Encourage students to comment on how this text feature affected how they understood the text.

RESPONSE OPTIONS

WRITING Have students write a fictional journal entry from the point of view of a spectator at Opening Day for the Brooklyn Dodgers in 1947. Prepare students by brainstorming idiomatic expressions used in sports commentary.

SOCIAL STUDIES CONNECTION

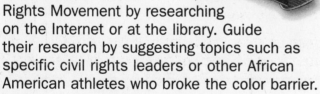

Students can learn more about the Civil Rights Movement by researching on the Internet or at the library. Guide their research by suggesting topics such as specific civil rights leaders or other African American athletes who broke the color barrier.

TEACH/REVIEW VOCABULARY

Have students practice finding the meaning of unfamiliar words by looking at the surrounding words and sentences for context clues. Begin with the word *segregated* at the top of page 5. Ask students to say the meaning in their own words and explain which context clues helped them understand the word. Repeat this process for remaining vocabulary.

TARGET SKILL AND STRATEGY

GENERALIZE Explain: When you read about several people, things, or ideas that are alike, you can make a *generalization* about them. Have students make and evaluate their own generalizations as they read. Group students in pairs; assign each a section of the book and have them write a generalization about their section. Next, have pairs trade statements and evaluate each other's statement by looking at facts from the text and thinking about their own experiences. Allow time to discuss all of the generalizations and the supporting facts.

PREDICT/CONFIRM PREDICTIONS Have students *predict* how Jackie will be treated in major league baseball. Write predictions on the board. Then have students read. As their predictions are *confirmed* as correct or incorrect, pause and encourage class discussion. Discuss how making predictions can help readers make generalizations.

ADDITIONAL SKILL INSTRUCTION

COMPARE AND CONTRAST Have students read page 5 and *compare* and *contrast* the two groups of baseball players. Draw a Venn diagram and complete it as group. Ask: How are the groups alike? How are they different? Next to the Venn diagram, write a list of clue words that helped students identify similarities and differences. Point out that the author did not use many clue words in the comparison.

Generalize

- To **generalize** is to make a broad statement or rule that applies to many examples.
- When you make a generalization, you look for similarities or differences among facts and examples in the text.

Directions Read the following passage. Then answer the questions below.

After he retired from baseball, Jackie and his wife Rachel participated in voter registration drives to register African American voters. They raised money to support Martin Luther King, Jr.'s organization, the Southern Christian Leadership Conference (SCLC). Jackie spoke out against segregation and tried to get other athletes involved in the Civil Rights Movement. He once said, "A life is not important except for the impact it has on other lives." Jackie's life was dedicated to service.

What generalization did the author make about Jackie's life?

1. _____

What four facts and examples from the passage support the generalization?

2. _____

3. _____

4. _____

5. _____

Directions Write your own generalization about Jackie Robinson. Then write four examples that support the generalization.

Generalization:

6. _____

Supporting examples:

7. _____

8. _____

9. _____

10. _____

130

Name _____

Vocabulary

Directions Synonyms are words that have similar meanings. Draw a line to match the synonyms.

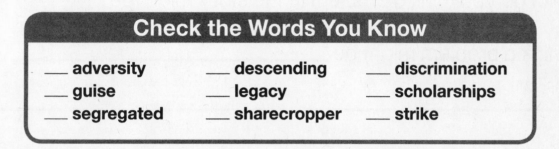

Check the Words You Know

___ adversity   ___ descending   ___ discrimination
___ guise   ___ legacy   ___ scholarships
___ segregated   ___ sharecropper   ___ strike

1. discrimination

2. guise

3. strike

4. scholarships

5. legacy

a. protest—an act that shows disapproval

b. heritage—lasting customs of a group of people

c. awards—prizes given for achievement

d. bias—unfair dislike

e. charade—a false act

Directions Antonyms are words that have the opposite meaning. Draw a line to match the antonyms.

6. adversity

7. descending

8. discrimination

9. segregated

10. sharecropper

f. planter—a plantation owner

g. integrated—to become joined or combined

h. ascending—moving upward

i. privilege—a special advantage or right

j. easiness—without challenge

© Pearson Education 3

Story Prediction from Previewing

Title _____

Read the title and look at the pictures in the story.
What do you think a problem in the story might be?

I think a problem might be _____

_____

_____

After reading _____ ,
draw a picture of one of the problems in the story.

Story Prediction from Vocabulary

Title and Vocabulary Words

Read the title and the vocabulary words.
What do you think this story might be about?

I think this story might be about _____

_____

_____

After reading _____ ,
draw a picture that shows what the story is about.

KWL Chart

Topic _____

What We **K**now	What We **W**ant to Know	What We **L**earned

Vocabulary Frame

_____
Word

_____
Association or Symbol

Predicted definition: _____

_____

One good sentence:

_____

_____

_____

Verified definition: _____

_____

_____

Another good sentence:

_____

_____

_____

Story Predictions Chart

Title _____

What might happen?	What clues do I have?	What did happen?

Story Sequence A

Title _____

Beginning

Middle

End

Story Sequence B

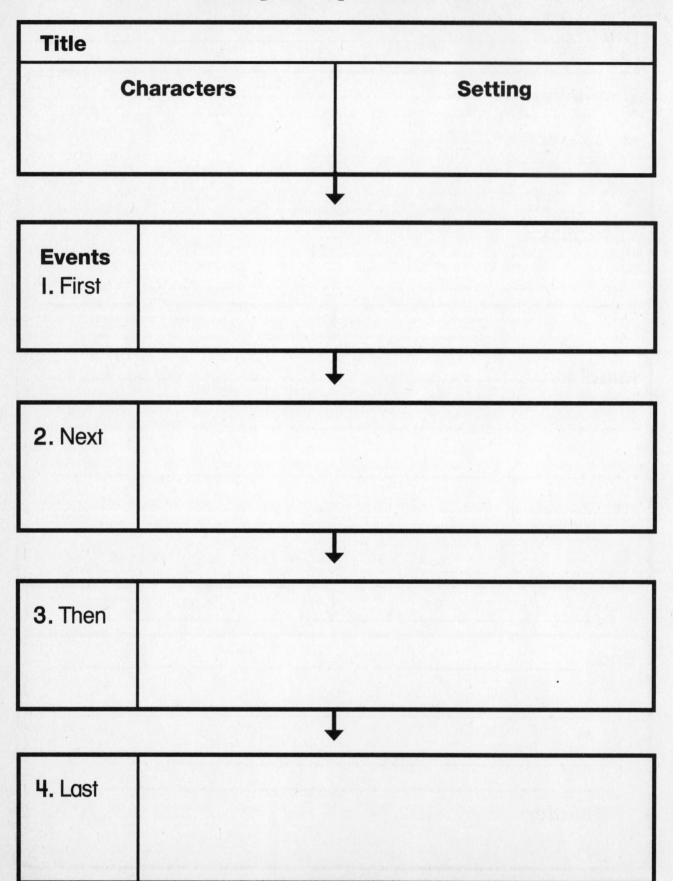

Title	
Characters	**Setting**

Events
1. First

2. Next

3. Then

4. Last

Story Sequence C

Title

Characters

Problem

Events

_____

_____

_____

_____

_____

_____

_____

_____

Solution

Question the Author

Title _____

Author _____ **Page** _____

1. What does the author tell you?	
2. Why do you think the author tells you that?	
3. Does the author say it clearly?	
4. What would make it clearer?	
5. How would you say it instead?	

Story Comparison

Title A _____

_____

Title B _____

_____

Characters	Characters

Setting	Setting

Events	Events

Web

Main Idea

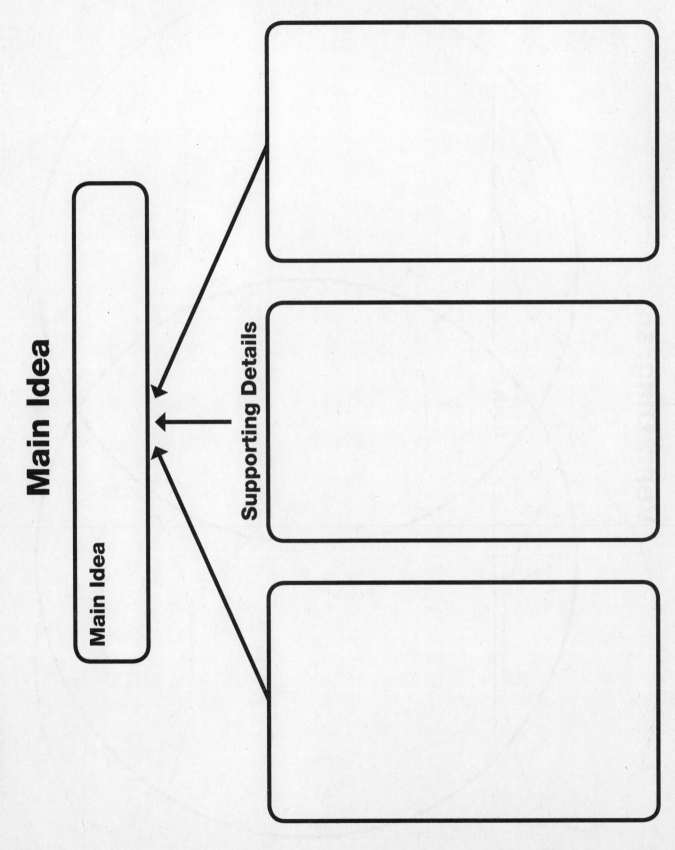

Main Idea

Supporting Details

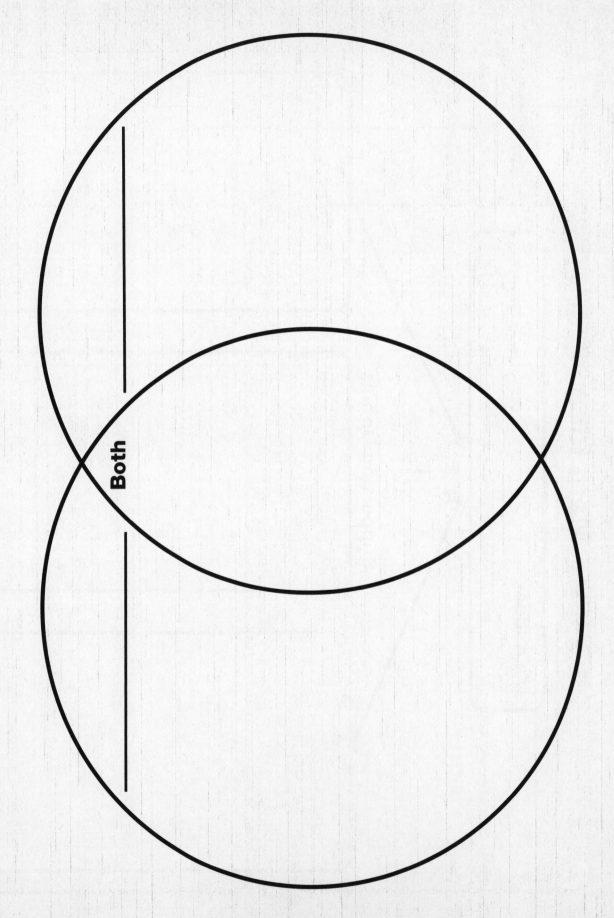

Venn Diagram

Both

Compare and Contrast

Topics

Alike

Different

Cause and Effect

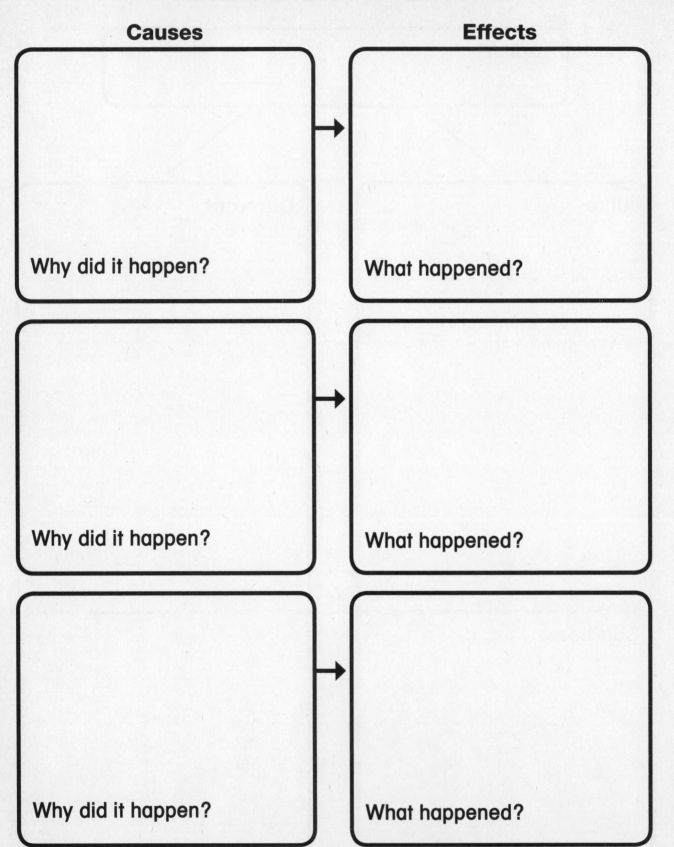

Causes

Effects

Why did it happen?

What happened?

Why did it happen?

What happened?

Why did it happen?

What happened?

© Pearson Education

Problem and Solution

Problem

Attempts to Solve the Problem

Solution

Time Line

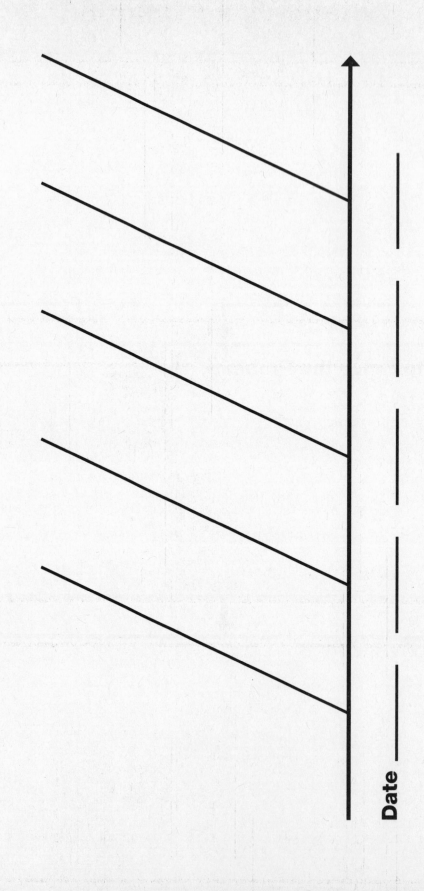

Date _____

Steps in a Process

Process _____

┌───┐
│ **Step 1**   │
│   │
│   │
│   │
└───┘
                        ↓
┌───┐
│ **Step 2**   │
│   │
│   │
│   │
└───┘
                        ↓
┌───┐
│ **Step 3**   │
│   │
│   │
│   │
└───┘

Three-Column Chart

Four-Column Chart

Four-Column Graph

Title _____

Answer Key

Leveled Reader Practice Pages

Mr. Post's Class p. 14
🔄 **REALISM AND FANTASY**
1. realism
Possible responses given for 2–5.
2. The paragraph describes activities that could happen in many communities.
3. start a recycling program; help the elderly bring home groceries; rake leaves for people
4. Yes. Parents often want to do volunteer work and help their children.
5. Mr. Post, the new teacher, was a frog, and he wanted to help the elephants in the neighborhood gather wood chips.

Mr. Post's Class p. 15 Vocabulary
1. organization
2. enthusiasm
3. volunteer
4. reporter
5. community
6. labor
7. mural
8. nonprofit
9. sign-up
10. success
Paragraphs will vary.

What's Money All About? p. 18
🔄 **SEQUENCE**
1. People decide what they want to trade; people bargain and/or compromise; the trade is either made or not.
2. The Egyptians sent stones, copper, grain, and papyrus to the Lebanese and received fir, cedar, and pine in return.
3. People set out what they want to trade. They decide if the trade is fair, and they take items or bring new ones.
4. First people bartered with goods. Then they used things like salt and wampum as currency. Last, people decided to use coins because they were easy to carry.
5. People were trading worldwide, and they needed a common system of money other than salt.

What's Money All About? p. 19 Vocabulary
Nouns: bargaining, compromise, currency, mints, wampum,
Verbs: bargaining, compromise, mints
1. e
2. a
3. b
4. d
5. c

Maggie McGee and Me at the Mint p. 22
🔄 **SEQUENCE**
Possible responses given. First, Sam and Nathan get a plan for sharing the game. Next, they ask their parents to buy the game. Next, their parents say they have to buy the game themselves. Then, they open a lemonade stand. Finally, they make enough money to buy the game themselves.

Maggie McGee and Me at the Mint
p. 23 Vocabulary
1. engrave
2. replicas
3. grooves
4. recited
5. precious
6. brainstormed, engrave, recited
7. detectors, grooves, replicas
8. detectors, grooves, replicas
Responses will vary.

Mr. Grim and the Goose p. 26
🔄 **REALISM AND FANTASY**
1. Mr. Grim lives in a house. He has a backyard with flowers, grass, and a pond. He has apple and pear trees.
2. Realistic: You can use gold to buy things like food, machinery, costumes, and building materials. Fantasy: Gold doesn't come in eggs.
3. It is a good idea to invest your money; you should be grateful for what you have and not be greedy for more.
4. Realistic: The goose loves the water, lays eggs, and has feathers.
Unrealistic: The goose talks, lays golden eggs, and invests them.
5. Statements will vary.

Mr. Grim and the Goose p. 27 Vocabulary
1. gleamed
2. glittering
3. deposit
4. invest
5. stockbroker
6. mortgage
Sentences will vary.

Pizza with a Twist p. 30
🔊 CHARACTER AND SETTING
Possible responses given.
1. Ruby: She is confused. Bo: He is hungry. Jake: He is creative.
2. Russia: The characters were cold. Peru: Tomatoes come from Peru. Italy: Cheese comes from Italy. India: Basil comes from India. Greece: Oregano comes from Greece.
3. Greece smells like fish.
4. The market in Greece has many olives on display.
5. Peru sounds noisy, with many vendors calling all at once.

Pizza with a Twist p. 31 Vocabulary
ACROSS	DOWN
2. garlic	1. ingredients
6. awnings	3. confused
7. vendors	4. oregano
	5. bazaar

Penguins On Parade p. 34
🔊 MAIN IDEA
Possible responses given.
1. penguins and the Southern Hemisphere
2. The Southern Hemisphere is home to the world's penguins.
3. Penguins live on the Galapagos Islands, in Australia, New Zealand, Africa, South America, and islands that surround Antarctica.
4. There are many things emperor penguins do to stay warm.
5. They stand on heels; they huddle together.

Penguins On Parade p. 35 Vocabulary
1. incubate
2. rookery
3. blubber
4. down
5. molt
6. brood patch
7. crest
8. lose old feathers
9. a place where groups of birds gather to raise their young
10. a layer that protects animals from the cold

The Song Makers Go to Salem p. 38
🔊 CHARACTER
Possible responses given.
Tabitha—Trait: honest; Clue: told Abbey that she saw her take money; Trait: thoughtful; Clue: gently convinced Abbey to admit her theft
Abbey—Trait: trusting; Clue: believed that Tabitha gave her good advice; Trait: strong; Clue: stood up and admitted she stole money

The Song Makers Go to Salem p. 39 Vocabulary
1. solution
2. frantically
3. concentrate
4. suspect
5. anxious
6. relieved
7. erupted
Paragraphs will vary.

Collecting Dreams p. 42
🔊 MAIN IDEA
Possible responses given.
1. china; porcelain
2. English bone china is a special kind of porcelain.
3–4. Porcelain was first made in China, hundreds of years ago. About two hundred years ago, the English added ash to make a special kind of porcelain called bone china.
5–7. Responses will vary.

Collecting Dreams p. 43 Vocabulary
1. rim
2. credit
3. kaleidoscope
4. collectibles
5. suspiciously
6. fond
7. porcelain
8. propped
9. specialize

The Magic of Coyote p. 46
🔊 AUTHOR'S PURPOSE
Possible responses given.
1. to entertain with a story of how a boy conquered his fear of dogs
2. This story informs, or explains, how humans got fire.
3. Henry likes the story about the coyote, which is similar to a dog, and it makes him less afraid of dogs.
4. She wants to inform readers about their rich tradition of storytelling.
5. Henry already liked coyotes, so it was easier to like the dog part of the coydog.

The Magic of Coyote p. 47 Vocabulary
1. yelping
2. retreated
3. artifacts
4. descendant
5. cunning
6. scampered
7. breakthrough
Possible responses given.
8. withdrew
9. a significant advance
10. making sharp, shrill cries or barks

Houses Past and Present p. 50

1. c   2. c
3. Possible response: Sod houses were not very comfortable, but the settlers worked well with the materials they had.
4. Possible response: The trees could be used for lumber, which would have made stronger, wooden houses.

Houses Past and Present p. 51 Vocabulary

1. thatch
2. tallow
3. puncheon
4. kilns
5. mortise
6. wattle
7. tenon
8. daub
9. pug mill

Sentences will vary but should correctly use some vocabulary words.

Nicky's Meadow p. 54

CAUSE AND EFFECT

1. f   3. a   5. h   7. g
2. b   4. c   6. e   8. d

Nicky's Meadow p. 55 Vocabulary

Possible responses given.
1. no longer used
2. fake
3. surprised
4. persuaded
5. miserable
6. a model of a person or animal made of material like clay
7. growing
8. walking with a swaying motion

Possible responses given.
9. He didn't want to leave Ohio and move to New York City.
10. There were gardens on top of the roofs. There was a castle in Central Park.
11. New York had a meadow and many other interesting things after all.

Star Tracks p. 58

AUTHOR'S PURPOSE

Possible responses given.
1. to inform the reader that this book is about the stars and how they help guide us
2. Columbus was a good example of how early sailors navigated using the equipment and knowledge that was available to them.
3. that early explorers depended on the sun, the moon, and the stars to guide them

4. After the sun went down, explorers had only the moon and the stars to guide them.
5. that he saw that the moon was rough and no one believed him; that he discovered Jupiter's moons; that he discovered that Venus traveled around the Sun, not the Earth

Star Tracks p. 59 Vocabulary

constellations, latitude, refractive, quadrant, celestial navigation, telescope, light-year, astronomers, galaxy, dead reckoning

Follow Me! How People Track Animals p. 62

DRAW CONCLUSIONS

Possible responses given.
1. John is afraid of dogs.
2. The weather is cold.
3. Zelda wanted to make sure she understood the story.

Responses will vary.

Follow Me! How People Track Animals p. 63 Vocabulary

1. a; someone who studies life
2. a; to spend the winter in a slowed-down, sleeping condition
3. a; information
4. a; living creature who feeds its young milk, has hair on its body, and does not lay eggs
5. b; to look at something critically

Whales and Other Animal Wonders p. 66

GENERALIZE

Possible responses given.
1. Some get stuck in marsh grass in a bay.
2. Some get trapped in narrow channels.
3. Today's large ships use noisy propellers.
4. Sonar may disrupt whales when they echolocate.
5. With fewer wolves, the number of coyotes increased.
6. More coyotes means less food for hawks.
7. Both warn people about dangers by barking.
8. Both protect people.
9. Wahoe, a chimpanzee, can "speak" using sign language.
10. Koko, a gorilla, has two cats as her pets.

Whales and Other Animal Wonders p. 67 Vocabulary

1. f   5. g
2. h   6. a
3. b   7. e
4. d   8. c

Possible response: A whale is a fascinating cetacean. As a species, the ability of whales to use echolocation has kept marine biologists studying them for many years. Some of these scientists have come to suspect that sonar may disrupt the whales.

Earth Movement p. 70
COMPARE AND CONTRAST
1. can't be predicted
2. can happen anywhere
3. natural disasters
4. change the shape of land
5. can be predicted
6. eruptions

Earth Movement p. 71 Vocabulary
DOWN	ACROSS
1. volcanologist	5. fumes
2. monitor	6. network
3. prehistoric	7. fault
4. observatory	8. magma
	9. instrument

Extraordinary Lives p. 74
CAUSE AND EFFECT
Cause: looking at the sun through a telescope;
Effect: loses his eyesight.
Cause: losing his eyesight;
Effect: Now people know not to look at the Sun through a telescope.
Cause: talking about his discovery even though it is against the law;
Effect: has to stay inside his house for the rest of his life

Extraordinary Lives p. 75 Vocabulary
1. pioneer
2. dedication
3. triumph
4. courageous
5. opportunities
6. appreciated
7. struggled
8. feats
9. prejudice
10. extraordinary

Fastest, Longest p. 78
COMPARE AND CONTRAST
1. a frying pan
2. Possible response: I can picture a frying pan in my mind and imagine a spider the same size.
3. a car
4. Possible response: I know that cars can go very fast, so I know that the cosmopolitan sailfish can go very fast too.
5. Possible response: The author compared something new to something familiar. It helped me understand what is special about the biggest spider and the fastest fish.

Fastest, Longest p. 79 Vocabulary
1. trivia
2. compendium
3. verified
4. accomplishment
5. procedure
6. verified
7. superlative
8. accomplishment
9. translated
10. existing

A Gem of a Tale! p. 82
GENERALIZE
Possible responses given.
1. Most gems are formed from minerals.
2. Minerals must cool and harden into crystal.
3. When first discovered, gems look like rocks.
4. They are often rough and unevenly shaped.
5. Gemstones are like snowflakes.
6. No two are exactly the same.

A Gem of a Tale! p. 83 Vocabulary
1. crystal
2. brilliant
3. transparent
4. flaws
5. rockhounds
6. birthstone
7. quartz
8. mined

A Time of Change p. 86
FACT AND OPINION
Possible responses given.
1. In 1920, a new law gave women the right to vote.
2. Most women did not mind working at home. It is the author's belief about women and cannot be checked in a source.
3. Oberlin College opened its doors to both men and women in 1833.
4. Of course, it was not easy for these women.
5. Fact: Many women choose to stay at home. Opinion: The most important job of all is being a mother.

A Time of Change p. 87 Vocabulary
Possible responses given.
1. prejudice, -ed, Martin Luther King, Jr., fought against prejudice
2. criticize, -ed, People should not criticize each other's clothing.
3. accept, -ed, Sometimes you have to accept the punishment for something you did.
4. opportunity, -ies, I took the opportunity to go to the amusement park on a free pass.
5. limit, -ed, It is a good idea to try to limit how much chocolate you eat.